From Pr

to Process

Stories from The National Assembly for Wales

Edited by Aled Edwards

Front cover photograph courtesy of the *Western Mail* and *South Wales Echo*.

ISBN 1 85994 459 0
Printed in Wales

Published by:
Cyhoeddiadau'r Gair, Cyngor Ysgolion Sul Cymru,
Ysgol Addysg, PCB, Safle'r Normal,
Bangor, Gwynedd, LL57 2PX.

Contents

'Our perception does not identify the outside world as it really is, but rather the way we are allowed to recognise it...'

Jorge Martins de Oliveira

From Protest to Process

Establishing a Shared Narrative

By Aled Edwards

My most memorable Assembly moment, and I have had many over the past four years, occurred one damp November afternoon on the cold and wired landing of A Wing in Cardiff Prison. It was quite a strange place to have an Assembly moment. It was also a shared experience as, for me, all good Assembly moments are.

I had spent the afternoon with Jane Hutt, Wales' Health and Social Services Minister, visiting the prison. Our main reason for being there that afternoon was to hold a much needed conversation with some of the asylum detainees who had been detained in the prison. The first group had been placed there some nine months earlier in February 2001. We knew by the time of our visit, following public assurances from the Home Office, that they would not be kept there long, but it was important towards the end of a process to hear their story.

Much to the embarrassment of all concerned, particularly the prison staff, by the time our small party arrived at A Wing the detainees had been taken elsewhere. The very last set of Cardiff's asylum detainees had been removed by officials a few days and even hours before our arrival. We were surprised. So were many of their legal representatives. I was pleased for them that they had been, at long last, removed from cramped cells in a Victorian building. However, I still felt a gut wrenching sense of loss knowing that I would never again see some people I had come to know rather well. Such political processes, alas, do not allow for farewell conversations.

After campaigning for several months for the removal of the detainees, I was also delighted that a new and very Welsh political process had achieved the desired result. Back in April, a cobbled together body called the Cardiff and District Asylum Network had been formed. Under the initiative of key individuals such as Shelagh Croskery of the Cardiff Law Centre, it included a number of faith communities, international charities, politicians and very active members of asylum pressure groups. It received considerable political support from Assembly Members such as Edwina Hart, William Graham, Jenny Randerson and Helen Mary Jones. Members of Parliament such as Julie Morgan and Ann Clwyd also helped press the case at Westminster. The network itself could so easily have been yet another useless cog in a Welsh lobbying culture already over blessed by an abundance of small groups with big names. It achieved its goal mainly by moving political protest through a process. That process, from my perspective, expressed itself for the most part through the National Assembly for Wales. The Assembly part of the story is told in this book by Helen Mary Jones.

The Network had, during the spring, protested outside the prison through high profile events such as vigils. Political protests clearly still have their place and the Welsh press and media, to their credit, also played a crucial part by refusing to see the story through the same politically tinted glasses as some of their London based press colleagues.

However, if truth really be known, the removal of Cardiff Prison's detainees was gained mainly through a quiet, robust and patient behind the scene political process at the Assembly. Protest may well have its place, but if it is to achieve results it has to be matched by conversation and process.

The story of the Cardiff Prison asylum detainees provides a vivid example of how devolution has made a difference to people's lives even in the context of a non-devolved issue such as immigration. To this day, particularly in the case of the detainees who had fallen under considerable bouts of depression, I believe that an uniquely Welsh political conversation may well have saved lives. I was with some of the detainees in August, 2001 when they brought their limited but desperate hunger strike to an end. The process certainly improved the lot of some of Wales' most vulnerable individuals.

This story is not exceptional. Since the advent of Welsh devolution in May, 1999 there have been many such Assembly moments. Some have been noted; a few have become stories; a very small number have become part of a nation's shared narrative. For a number of reasons, an extensive calendar of Assembly moments have simply been missed by a culture. For me, as a full time Assembly watcher, they stand out as rather embarrassing unkept engagements with a people.

The purpose of this book is simply to present an array of Assembly stories. They have been provided, with an election looming, as building blocks for a more creative conversation around Welsh politics. Most are told by individuals who have been actively engaged with a political process, but who are not politicians or journalists. The four Assembly Members who have written stories or reflections were asked to write as individuals. All the contributors have been invited to tell their personal story because they have achieved things. They have been asked to reflect on that personal achievement or to tell its story.

Why then, gather these building blocks for a shared narrative? I have to concede that the first reason flows from a deep personal frustration over a four year period of having to listen, mainly around the Assembly's milling area, to so many good stories just before they vanished into the political ether. The preacher in me has always wanted to turn events into stories. Over the years, this 'vanishing' has adopted many faces. I offer just four briefly as passing observations.

First, there have been the events that have simply never developed into stories. For the people of Gwynedd, for example, one of the most significant debates in the institution's early history occurred in March, 2000. The Assembly had been asked to approve a draft order concerning the Dinorwig and Ffestiniog power stations. Phil Williams of Plaid Cymru claimed that the initial level of rating for pump storage had been set too high by the Department of the Environment, Transport and the Regions (DETR) at £36,000 per mega watt. If the DETRs levels had been applied to Wales the pump storage schemes in Ffestiniog and Dinorwig would have faced an additional £6 million. It was claimed by Phil Williams (2000) that the future of one of the plants could well have been threatened by such an increase. The Assembly, using its powers, cut the rating assessment to just over a third of the initial rate.

Of itself, the incident provides a valuable example of an early engagement with the DETR where the Assembly acted on behalf of a key industry in north Wales and delivered. Yet, it was an event that never became a story. I doubt very much whether my former school mates in Blaenau Ffestiniog ever got to hear of it or my former parishioners in Dinorwig.

Secondly, there have been the really good stories that have failed to mature into conversation pieces. The involvement of Welsh civil servants in the UK-wide BSE and CJD issues provide an interesting case in point.

Pre devolution, during the BSE crisis, Whitehall ignored Welsh Office advice concerning the Department of Health's reassurances over food safety. As the then Agriculture Minister, John Gummer, was feeding his daughter a beefburger, behind the scenes, Wales' chief medical officer, Dame Deidre Hine, was quite rightly voicing her concern about the Department of Health's attempts to re-assure the public that beef was safe. At the time, Welsh intervention brought a cool response from London. A senior medical officer at the Department of Health even felt that it was 'inappropriate' to discuss detailed scientific evidence with a Welsh Office colleague.

There was to be a more specific twist in the tail of the BSE story in November 2001. It was announced (Press Release 30 November, 2001) that Assembly officials had defended the Welsh sheep sector by identifying the need for further DNA testing of samples used on worrying failed research on BSE in sheep. The tests subsequently showed that the research by DEFRA had in fact been conducted on cow brain, rather than sheep brain material. It is difficult to imagine the cost to UK agriculture if pleas for a second test from National Assembly officials had been treated with the same contempt as during the original BSE investigation. This story failed to mature into a nation's shared narrative.

Thirdly, there have been the many whispered stories that should have been shouted from the rooftops and heeded within a more thorough Welsh political conversation. One of my lasting memories of observing the Assembly at work over its first two years was being able, through greater openness and accountability, to identify three Macbeth like witches hovering through the 'fog and filthy air' of Welsh deprivation. I did so with considerable concern.

There was the matter of EU money earmarked for Wales. The first two meetings of the Assembly's Economic Committee discovered that the Barnett Block, allocating money from the UK Treasury to Wales, did not contain a component covering EU money earmarked for Wales. The shortfall over a five-year period was estimated, at the time, at £250 million (Minutes: Economic Development Committee 16 and 30 June 1999).

During the same period, came the news of the overall effect of under investment in health spending. By the end of the financial year 1998-99, the Health Authorities and Trusts in Wales had built up cumulative deficits of some £72 million (Minutes: Health and Social Services Committee 21 July, 1999). The publication of the new Policy Unit's *Stocktake of NHS Wales* allowed a debate by the Assembly's Health and Social Services Committee on the role of the internal market and the adequacy of funding in the light of poorer health levels in Wales. The deficit was also cleared.

There was also the issue of under investment by UK charities in Wales. At the March 2001 meeting of the Voluntary Sector Partnership Council Meeting (VSPC), Karen Ingram of the Wales Funders Forum indicated, on the basis of the available data, that there were some 8,800 trusts and foundations in the UK. They had, at the time, distributed £1.25 billion to charities and voluntary groups. Of this, only £10 million seems to have been given to Wales (Minutes: VSPC Meeting 16 March 2001). Further research is currently being undertaken concerning this rather 'silent' charity investment gap. It's particularly pleasing in this work, to record how the ARC Addington Fund bucked this trend by allocating, at the height of the Foot and Mouth crisis, some 33% of its UK grant distribution to Wales.

Sadly, the story of such massive under investing in a largely deprived nation, measured in hundreds of millions, has rarely spilled over into a shared narrative. In terms of story telling, it will always be easier to add some Assembly expenditure figures and divide them by sixty to create a newspaper headline. All too frequently, the telling of the Assembly story has been burdened by a malignant priority setting predilection towards 'straining out a gnat and swallowing a camel' (Matthew 23:24).

Rather typically perhaps, Wales has at times been remarkably slow in blowing its own trumpet about how devolution has been worked out, for example, in meeting the needs of deprived communities. The Welsh Communities First Regeneration Scheme differs significantly from the English Neighbourhood Renewal Strategy. One is not comparing kind with kind, but certain key comparisons deserve observation All authorities in Wales have at least one community included in the programme while in England just over a quarter of the authorities were deemed eligible. Wales has identified not only the 100 most deprived communities at electoral division level, but also 32 smaller communities marked as pockets of deprivation at sub electoral division level and a further 10 communities of special interest. This process has allowed support to be given to areas that would not otherwise have been supported. Centralisation in Cardiff, I would contend, is largely a myth.

Finally, there have been the many conversations that have just stuttered under the overwhelming chatter of the much louder UK based media hegemonies. Professor Jorge Martins de Oliveira (1997) made the discerning point from the world of neuroscience, that 'our perception does not identify the outside world as it really is, but rather the way we are allowed to recognise it.' The same may be said of perceptions concerning Wales' infant legislature.

More often than not, the London based press and media have just ignored distinctives brought about by the Assembly – especially the very good ones. This was certainly the case when a consequential spin off of some £600 million flowed towards the more deprived areas of England following the very Welsh Objective One debate in July 2000. Gordon Brown's (2000) comments in his statement before the House of Commons on the Spending Review are worth quoting:

> For objective 1 areas in the United Kingdom - in Wales, Cornwall, Merseyside and South Yorkshire - and for objective 2 and 3 areas, I am today announcing a new approach that will raise their levels of

investment ... the Government will ensure funding for the European share of objective 1, 2 and 3 projects. For European Union structural funds, that is estimated to total £4.2 billion over three years, including an estimated total of £600 million for new objective 1 programmes in English regions.

At the time, it appeared to this rather ardent Assembly watcher, that sections of the London based press and media could not see Welsh devolution in a generous light because they were not culturally equipped to do so. Dare I suggest that sections of the same cultural hegemony would find it equally difficult in August 2002 to pass generous comment on a rather clever Welsh Archbishop who could command the seat of Canterbury and, like the Queen, be a member of the *Gorsedd* of bards?

The main reason for collecting these stories however, flows from another memorable Assembly moment associated with the Archbishop. The reason offers a more substantial case than personal frustration.

During the summer of 2002, an official, deep from somewhere within the entrails of the Cathays Park building in Cardiff, had a really good idea. That, in my experience, happens a little more often than many dare concede. I was asked if Rowan Williams, the then Archbishop of Canterbury designate, would possibly accept an invitation to address some of the Assembly's officials in the Angel Hotel, Cardiff, during a day event in late September. Thankfully, he was both free and willing.

In his address, Rowan Williams (2002) explored the role of nations, markets and morals. Others would later hear an enhanced version of his contribution in the 2002 Richard Dimbleby Lecture. He opened a piercing analysis by exploring why people should now accept the legitimacy of a particular political system - whether that be in Wales or elsewhere. Being fully aware of the unspoken contracts that people feel exist between themselves and their rulers, he suggested that we are now living in a period where the basic assumptions, about how states work, are shifting. The view that we are witnessing the replacing of the nation state with the market state is being increasingly canvassed.

Taking his lead from the American strategist and historian, Philip Bobbitt (2002), the Archbishop offered an analysis of what shifting towards a market state means in our current culture, where Welsh homes and timber built bars in Kampala exercise a shared function as variable boxes at the bottom of TV satellite dishes. Increasingly in such a global - market driven world, it seems that what makes a government, even a devolved government, worth obeying or having, is its ability to clear a space for individuals or groups to do their own negotiating and to pursue what they want. The consumerist model in education, for example, with its emphasis on parental choice and the publication of results has, according to Rowan Williams (2002), allowed the 'actual philosophy of education itself to be obscured behind a cloud of sometimes mechanical criteria of attainment.' The willingness in Wales to abandon league tables issues a significant cry against the consumerist model. It hints significantly, I would suggest, at a different way of being state.

What then, of the National Assembly? If Wales is to dive headlong into the market state model, the Assembly's legitimacy will constantly be questioned. It was born, it would seem, into an unwelcoming consumerist world. At elections, its power to buy the Welsh electorate's way out of insecurity will always be limited as will its capacity to provide instant answers to instant demands.

For me, as a committed devolutionist, the Assembly's legitimacy rests not on its ability to compete in a consumer driven market, but in the offering of an alternative to that model. The stories included in this book, in many ways, hold conversations around the large gaps in society left by the consumerist model of what a state is. They hint, within a modern Welsh context, at a different way of being state.

For Rowan Williams (2002), there is a substantial worry. I share it. If, in the marketised world we are left to make the best decisions for ourselves what of the larger story? As he states: 'People learn how to tell the story of their own lives in a coherent way when they have some broader picture to which to relate it. You can only tell the story of your own life, it seems, when it isn't just your story, or even the story of those immediately close to you.' The stories in this book speak of shared experiences around human values in all their diverse complexity. The accumulated narrative dares to see people as being more than individual customers in a market and looks towards the Assembly, as an expression of government, to allow society to retain some shape.

Wales has good stories to tell but if communities are to share a better conversation and participate in a more effective political process, far more stories will have to be told and they will have to be told well.

Aled Edwards was brought up in Trawsfynydd in Gwynedd and was the parish priest of Llandinorwig and Penisarwaun, Botwnnog and Dewi Sant, Cardiff, before becoming the Churches' National Assembly Liaison Officer in May 1999. He is married with three grown up children and used to like Star Trek before indulging a greater passion for West Wing. He is also chair of the Cardiff and District Asylum Network .

With Right on Your Side

The Campaign to Extend the Homelessness Law in Wales

By John Puzey

Director of Shelter Cymru

Some of us believe that the *Homelessness (Priority Need) (Wales) Order 2001* has been the most significant secondary legislation the Welsh Assembly has so far passed. It has extended help to many more homeless people, (almost 2,000 extra homeless households have already benefited from it in the first year), it marked a new 'made in Wales' approach to homelessness, it gave a clear signal about a real intent to challenge social exclusion from a rights perspective, and it would have been inconceivable under the old Welsh Office regime.

When the TV drama *Cathy Come Home* disturbed the post war 'you never had it so good' consensus in 1966, two related things occurred. The charity Shelter was born and the concept that homelessness is primarily about the lack of a home, began to gain ground. Sounds strange? Well this was the time when housing officers, without irony, responded to homelessness surveys by asking – what's it got to do with us? Homelessness was entirely a behavioural issue with a 'poor law' response. Homeless families were split, mother and child usually placed in a hostel under the National Assistance Act, with the possibility of the child being taken into care if the family could not find alternative accommodation.

For those who were not around then, or can't remember, the public shock of *Cathy Come Home* revealing the existence of homelessness, squats and children being taken away from families for no other reason than they had no where to live, may be difficult to comprehend now, but then it was massive and created a 'something must be done' atmosphere which politicians began to reflect.

After a long campaign new legislation was introduced in 1977 that required local councils to re-house certain groups of homeless people, mainly households with dependent children. At the time campaigners saw the legislation as a necessary compromise - single homeless people and childless couples would not be fully assisted, they would get 'advice and help' only, local councils had 'get out' clauses which allowed them to find some people 'intentionally' homeless. But, as a first step, linking at last, housing to homelessness, it was rightly felt to be hugely important. The idea was, that gradually, the legislation would be amended to ensure that all homeless people got proper help. But it was an idea which ran into a different government and thinking in the 80's.

Before we go further, perhaps we should be clear about what is meant by the term homelessness. Most people have an image in their mind when they think about homelessness which probably includes cardboard cities, sleeping rough in shop doorways, begging and so on. The next thought, probably, is that it's a problem in London but you don't see too much of it in Wales. Let's be clear, all people who sleep rough are obviously homeless, but all people who become homeless do not necessarily sleep rough. In fact most don't.

The point is that many people in Wales live in temporary accommodation, perhaps hostels or bed and breakfast establishments, or live itinerant lives staying with friends and relatives, or live in accommodation that is so poor it is considered unfit for habitation. Many also face homelessness because they are on short term lets in the private rented sector, or are in rent or mortgage arrears, or are on insecure introductory council tenancies or have to leave overcrowded conditions.

To be homeless is to be without a home. A home is somewhere private, secure, healthy, warm . It's where you want to be, a place free from fear, a place where others cannot invade and remove you. The law recognises that you can have a roof over your head, but you may not have a home. In 2001, around 35,000 people in Wales asked their local councils for help because they felt they were homeless or were facing homelessness. Shelter Cymru believe that up to 50,000 people a year experience homelessness in Wales.

To be without a home is destructive – it ruins both physical and emotional health – it creates victims who cannot break out of the cycle of poverty and deprivation, it destroys relationships, it can ruin children's education, it affects the life chances of young people, it becomes harder to get a job, it can impoverish extended families and friends trying to help, it causes absences from work and school, it costs the NHS millions of pounds a year, it has an almost invisible destructive impact on the whole community.

People who sleep rough in particular are susceptible to disease, assault and early death. But research shows that anyone who is homeless and living in temporary accommodation is disproportionately likely to be affected by higher rates of depression, illness and suicide. Unsurprisingly evidence shows that former prisoners who find themselves homeless are six times more likely to re-offend that someone who finds a decent home. A young person who becomes homeless is more likely to fall victim to exploitation and abuse.

In Wales, since 1977, the provisions of the *Homeless Persons Act* has helped over a quarter of a million people. But there were three important caveats to this success story.

First the impact of the legislation began to be eroded by laws which started to reduce the duties of local councils to homeless people - laws passed in Westminster largely responding to housing problems in the south east of England and more specifically London. Secondly, the resources available to councils to carry out their duties to homeless people, in particular of course suitable rented accommodation, continued to decline.

Finally, tragically and ironically, the largest and most significantly growing group of homeless people were largely ignored by the legislation. The growth of single homelessness, particularly among 'young' single people was one of the most disturbing features of the 80's and 90's in Wales. It was the country's worst kept secret. Official figures did not record it – precisely because they were not entitled to the full duties under the Act – but everyone 'on the front line' knew it was happening.

Not only this – but it was also clear from surveys in Wales and the rest of the UK that certain groups of people, also not fully assisted by the law, were disproportionately found sleeping rough: people who had left care, former prisoners and ex-members of the armed forces and people who had left institutions unadvised and unprepared and who had found themselves without a home.

For many years organisations like Shelter Cymru had argued that young homeless people were particularly vulnerable and needed more help. Sometimes some councils did assist young people and others as the law allows discretion to consider potentially vulnerable people outside the normal 'priority groups'. But this was discretionary, hit and miss – and most young homeless people didn't bother to even try and get considered because they knew that the best they would probably get is a list of bed and breakfast establishments.

Shelter Cymru's efforts in Wales largely focused on supporting and representing young homeless people and other 'non-priority' homeless applicants trying to make individual cases for vulnerability, and supporting the efforts of other Welsh and UK organisations in trying to get the legal homeless safety net extended. It didn't look promising – but then a new government and the possibility of a Welsh Assembly gave the campaign a new lease of life. Getting the UK as a whole to change and be innovative might be a bit beyond Welsh organisations but Wales was institutionally small enough to be dynamic but big enough to make a difference to a lot of people's lives.

If the Assembly was going to both reflect the real issues in Wales and be innovative and bold, as well as putting the challenge of social exclusion at , or at least near the top of its agenda, what better starting point than the most socially excluded of all groups – people who become homeless.

The story of the new rights started in 1997 when the new Welsh Office regime appeared much more inclusive, inviting voluntary organisations and other agencies into discussions about the future of Welsh housing. Importantly it showed a readiness to develop a specific Welsh housing strategy for eventual adoption by the new Assembly.

At this time Shelter Cymru began to intensify its campaign, supported by Rough Sleepers Cymru, Housing Forum Cymru and many other housing and related organisations in Wales, to extend the homeless safety net to include a range of new but clearly vulnerable groups. Our preference was for all homeless people in Wales to become 'priority need', but for now we felt that was probably politically unrealistic and would be seen as contrary to the aims of the primary legislation. Secondary legislation, or statutory instruments, can develop primary legislation but it cannot contradict or undermine its primary aims. Nevertheless, it was clear that the primary legislation allowed potentially important changes to be effected in Wales if the political will allowed.

Despite the more inclusive nature of the Welsh office approach it was clear it was not ready to take any dramatically different legislative directions from England. For this to move forward we needed an Assembly with democratic accountability to Wales, and one which could be constructively lobbied with evidence and reason.

The case was simply stated – all the evidence showed that single young people and certain other groups of people leaving institutions, were particularly susceptible to homelessness in Wales and that legislation ensuring these groups of people had a right to the full re-housing duties under the law would dramatically tackle social exclusion. In addition, of course, it would increase work and education opportunities, improve health, reduce crime and so on. It would also help reinforce other legislation, such as the Children's Act, and it reflected some of the key challenges facing Wales already highlighted by the Assembly such as social inclusion and opportunities for young people. Most importantly the Assembly 'could' do something about it, and it could be done through its devolved legislative function - in other words it would be a 'rights' approach to confronting the issue, not only one of good practice and guidance.

The rights approach was vital. It meant that local authorities would have to accept people in the new categories ensuring a consistent approach across Wales. It is the best way to maximise take up, and it becomes in itself an effective tool for arguing for more resources. The rights approach also reinforces a set of principles and values that the most vulnerable and marginalised in our communities have a right to become full citizens of our country.

The possibility of addressing homelessness through statuary instruments in Wales would not have occurred if it was only one or two organisations calling for it. It is important to recognise that not only did a lobby of voluntary organisations begin to develop, but a number of Assembly Members and civil servants also started to see this as a possible approach.

A key factor for Assembly Members was a real desire to make a difference and to show that the Assembly could make a real impact on social exclusion and that it could do it differently from England. We are often asked what is so different about homelessness in Wales compared to England that requires this different approach. (In England any extension of duties will probably be discretionary for most of the new groups.) Our response is the difference is in what we can do about it.

The campaign was championed in the Assembly by Peter Black AM and a statutory instrument order was drafted which extended priority need in Wales under the *1996 Housing Act*, to 16 and 17 year olds, care leaves and people at particular risk of sexual or financial exploitation between 18 and 21, people fleeing actual or threatened domestic violence, people who become homeless after leaving the armed forces and people who become homeless after leaving prison.

The ride was not easy. It initially became mixed up with the pre-coalition politics at that time - with calls for the order to be delayed pending an England and Wales review of the homeless persons legislation. But it was finally approved in 2000 and began its consultative phase.

To be fair local councils in Wales largely accepted the need for the extension though made strong arguments, as they still do, about the lack of resources to properly respond to their new duties. But the process showed, in the end, an overwhelming level of support had been built for the move and all parties in the Assembly supported the *Homeless (Priority Need) (Wales) order 2001* which appropriately become law in Wales on St. David's Day 2001. Then came the little matter of implementation....but that's another book.

With the passing of the *Homelessness Act* in 2002 as well, which requires local councils to develop more holistic local homelessness strategies and a significant increase in Assembly funding for homelessness schemes, we are, in Wales, making real progress in the cause of ending homelessness, and the Assembly has been, and will continue to be, crucial in that work both in terms of funding and leading a new homelessness agenda.

But it is vital that new primary legislation continues to allow the scope for innovation and our ability to respond to Welsh conditions with Welsh solutions where appropriate. We all have a role in ensuring that devolved democracy is not strangled by centralist tendencies when it comes to drafting new laws. The innovative way in which the legislation has been used along with the development of a national homeless strategy for Wales has also began to catch the imagination in England - some agencies are beginning to see regional government in England in a whole new light.

The danger for us in the homelessness lobby is that we might think its all over - but we know its only the beginning. Housing overall still claims less than 6% of the Welsh budget which means that there is still major issues about conditions and the supply of quality rented accommodation in places where people need to live. Many homeless people still fall outside of full statutory help, even within the new groups more support and assistance to ensure they are able to maintain accommodation is needed, we want to end 'intentional homelessness', we want all homeless people to be offered greater opportunities to make choices and decisions over their own future, so there is a longer than ever agenda in the fight against homelessness. But we can all be proud that our first indigenous law in Wales reached out to our most vulnerable and marginalised citizens.

John Puzey has been the Director of Shelter Cymru since 1990. He was a member of the Welsh Homelessness Commission and is currently part of the Welsh Assembly Homelessness Strategy Working Party. He likes advice and guidance but prefers rights.

The Longest Waiting List of All

By Kirsty Williams

Welsh Liberal Democrat Assembly Member for Brecon and Radnorshire

Any politician who had been involved in the 1999 National Assembly Campaign was well versed in the issue of NHS waiting lists. They had been and still remain the topic that dominated the health and social care agenda.

However, in the summer that year, I attended a conference in my role as Chair of the Health and Social Services Committee that brought to my attention a group of patients that had never made the front page of a newspaper or TV headlines. Yet, this group of NHS patients had been waiting and waiting. Many had had their hopes and expectations raised only to see them dashed. Their waiting times would put that of orthopaedics in the shade, because for many of these patients they had been waiting a lifetime.

Since my election I had become accustomed to surprises; I had become accustomed to the huge amount of work that needed to be done by the National Assembly. However, nothing was as powerful and as compelling as 'The Longest Waiting List' Campaign that I was introduced to that day, in the Standing Conference of Voluntary Organisations for People with a Learning Disability in Wales (SCOVO) sponsored conference in Llandrindod Wells.

Representatives of SCOVO and a number of People First Groups carefully explained that some patients with a range of learning difficulty still found themselves living in long stay hospitals in south and north Wales. This was despite earlier commitments to close all such hospitals and provide accommodation and support of varying degrees in the community. The policy had seen many patients successfully housed and the closure of out of date institutions. However, in 1999 the policy had ground to a standstill, with patients still residing in Hensol, Llanfrechfa Grange in south Wales and Bryn-y-Neuadd, north Wales.

It is impossible to stereotype the patients who remained in hospital. Over the year, well meaning professionals had advised parents and relatives, that their loved ones could be cared for better in such institutions. Often, those patients had learning difficulties combined with health problems. However, sometimes in the past, so-called 'feckless' individuals and unmarried girls who found themselves pregnant had found themselves admitted. For some, practically their entire lives had been lived out on these institutionalised wards.

Of course, by 1999 medical practise had changed, and different ways of providing care, support and educational opportunities had been developed in community settings. But, in 1999 there were still over 300 people, effectively incarcerated, in hospital wards, when all they wanted and needed was a place to live that they could call a home.

This led to me tabling a Statement of Opinion on 22 September 1999 (OPIN-1999-0035

Putting an End to the Longest Waiting List of All):

> This Assembly recognises that all people with a learning disability have: A right to an ordinary pattern of life in the community; A right to be treated as an individual; and a right to the additional help and support in developing their maximum potential, therefore the Assembly fully supports the completion of the resettlement programme for people with learning disabilities, over 300 of whom currently reside in long stay hospitals.

The 'rightness' of the policy of resettlement was made real to me by a young woman who came to tell her story to Assembly Members in February 2000, at a meeting of the All Party Resettlement Monitoring Group. She had a learning disability. She had lived at Hensol Hospital for many years. She then moved into her own flat in Bridgend in the first part of the resettlement programme. Her story was an eye opener. She was nervous at speaking in front of all these so-called 'important' people. She needn't have worried – she had the entire audience spellbound.

Every day activities that we all take for granted were a wonder for this young woman and her friends. To be able to get up when she wanted, to go to the shops when she wanted, to eat when and what she liked, to go to the pub with friends and above all, take care of her beloved pet cats. She had not been able to do any of it whilst in hospital. She now was an active member of her local People First Group, an organisation that campaigns for the improvement of services and empowerment of people with learning difficulties.

To find out more, I arranged to visit both Hensol and Llanfrechfa Grange. The staff and nurses of the hospitals worked hard to provide a good level of care. But, efforts could not hide the fact that these patients were living in hospitals when really they needed to live as independently as possible. One ward, to me, resembled something I can only describe as being akin to pictures from Romanian orphanages that had filled our screens some years earlier. It was shocking to think people were living and working in those conditions, here in Wales.

In another ward, the staff had decorated, but no amounts of floral wallpaper, gingham curtains at the windows and floor mats could disguise the fact we were in a hospital ward. As I entered the ward escorted by a host of NHS managers, an elderly gentleman approached. Standing in front of me he shouted into my face "F*** Off". Colour flared up in the manager's faces; they began to apologise profusely. I told them to forget it. I told them that if some stranger walked uninvited into my home, I'd say exactly the same.

There was no way that I could forget it. With the help of those inside and outside the Assembly we continued to lobby the Minister, Jane Hutt. These people might not make the headlines, they may not be a 'sexy' political issue, but they needed a hand. People with learning disabilities should be able to live in a world where they have security, dignity and choice.

In December 1999 the National Assembly established the Learning Disability Advisory Group to prepare a draft national service framework for people with learning disabilities.

This framework would cover all services and support available to people with learning disabilities, whatever their age or the severity of their disability. This resulted in the much awaited report entitled *Fulfilling the Promises* which came to the Assembly in 2001. One of the recommendations in the report was that the target date for the resettlement of people with learning difficulties should be brought forward from 2010 to 2006

Meanwhile in October 2000 the Partnership Government was formed between the Welsh Liberal Democrats and Labour and here was an opportunity to highlight the problems of people on the longest waiting list of all. I made the case, and the following pledge was made (2000):

> Over the lifetime of the Partnership Government, we will ensure that suitable accommodation in the community is made available for people with learning disabilities currently living in long-stay hospitals.

As a result of this pledge £60 million over 3 years was allocated by the Assembly for resettlement of people with learning disabilities in the community and in January 2001 Jane Hutt announced an additional £25 million. Then in July last year, after what seemed to many an interminably long wait, the report on *Fulfilling the Promises* was debated in the Assembly. I am pleased to say that the Minister then agreed to the recommendation to set a new target date for the completion of the resettlement programme to 2006.

So progress had at last been made. We brought home to many people that these people were not just statistics, but real people living real lives. As Eifion Jones, Chair of Mencap Cymru said so poignantly: "People with a learning disability, their families and carers, need support – not to live better lives than their friends and neighbours – but to live the same lives." I am proud that this National Assembly has striven to enable people with learning disabilities to live a dignified life in a setting of their own choosing. After all surely the measure of a civilised society is how we care for the vulnerable people within it.

Kirsty Williams was born in 1971 and was a marketing and PR executive before becoming an Assembly member. Kirsty was the Deputy President of the Welsh Liberal Democrats between 1997 – 1999 and was a member of the National Assembly Advisory Group. She is currently her party's spokesperson on health and social services.

Helmets and Cowboy Hats

A view of the Assembly's human rights achievements and challenges from under different brims

By Eleanor White

It seems congruent to introduce some hats other than my usual Amnesty International beret. I sport a well worn and somewhat tattered and torn mental health helmet, a Common Purpose mortar board, no doubt with multicoloured tassels and the rainbow shimmering diamond tiara of the Lesbian Gay and Bisexual movement in Wales (LGB). Actually, that last one's probably more accurately described as a cowboy hat.

What I hope to do is take the broad question, how has the Assembly Government addressed its commitment in *Better Wales* (2000) to a programme of reform, including 'support for those most in need' - thus fulfilling its obligations to comply with the European Convention on Human Rights (ECHR) and other conventions - and look at it in relation to the two areas of mental health and lesbian, gay and bisexual rights and needs.

Before the *Human Rights Act* came into force in October 2000, the National Assembly for Wales' compliance with the ECHR was provided for within the *Government of Wales Act 1998*. The areas within the ECHR that seem most relevant to both the mental health and the LGB movement are in particular, the prohibition of discrimination Article 14 of ECHR, also the rights of Article 5, Liberty and Security of Person, Article 8, Respect for Private and Family Life and Article 10, Freedom of Expression.

The aspirations of these two movements in some ways were not dissimilar; both seeking to end discrimination through improved services, better joint working, cross-sector communication and a better, positive profile in Wales. The ability of the Assembly to address such aspirations lies within its devolved policy making powers for equality, an imperative cross-cutting all devolved functions of the government, and for Health and Social Services translated into the formation and delivery of a separate strategy for Wales.

The positive duty to promote equality within the *Government of Wales Act 1998* was not confined to the three strands of race, gender and disability, but required the National Assembly for Wales to have 'due regard to the principle that there should be equality of opportunity for all people' (Section 120). It pronounced a welcome opportunity to all minority rights lobbies for the Assembly to interpret equality in its widest sense – which it famously did, with recognition of its 'absolute duty' to promote equality and adoption of equal opportunities as one of its three underlying principles of governance, along with social inclusion and sustainable development.

So, to take a more detailed look now, from under that dented mental health helmet: in addressing mental health issues the Assembly has been strong on vision, but not so strong (yet) on delivery. The white paper *Better Health, Better Wales* (1998), produced just before the Assembly came into existence, set out an approach to health policy, including mental health, which confronted discrimination and social exclusion and recognised the non-medical determinants of health such as poverty, discrimination and isolation. The paper stated that 'sustainable health is achieved when people and communities take control of their own lives' (3.1), a statement that would later inform the vision of the Welsh *Mental Health Strategy* (2001) and provide the ground for the Assembly's response to mental health law reforms proposed by Westminster, where a very different agenda later began to take root.

Early on, the Assembly identified the need for a mental health strategy and Jane Hutt, as Minister for Health and Social Services, emphasised that mental health should no longer be the 'Cinderella' of service provision. Evidence of an inheritance of 'Cinderella' services was (and is) not hard to come by as a string of reports from Joint Audits (Audit Commission and Social Services Inspectorate) into Local Authority provision and Health Advisory Service reports on Health provision painted a bleak picture of both community and clinical services. The Assembly responded by identifying mental health, along with cancer and heart care, as one of the three health priorities for its first term.

The Assembly's *Adult Mental Health Strategy* (launched 25 September 2001 – Press Release) embodies in its vision the same focus on empowerment and equity that animate *Better Health, Better Wales* (1998), however the document and subsequent implementation plan have been criticised for lacking the detailed planning to follow this through. There is a lack of baseline assessment, a weakness for hazy target setting and critically, an absence of costing and resourcing the implementation process. A further challenge to hopes for radical improvement in the provision of mental health services in Wales has been the controversial decision to restructure Health Services in Wales by replacing 8 Local Health Authorities with 22 Local Health Boards. However this pans out (supporters of the proposal argue that it brings commissioning and planning closer to communities, critics argue that it creates duplication, bureaucracy and expense and undermines strategies which aim to give a consistent standard of healthcare across Wales) the initial impact may have been to paralyse some processes of planning and to absorb resources crucial to the implementation of the mental health and other strategies.

Although the Assembly has struggled to match vision to delivery, the strong value base expressed in the strategy and other documents has helped Wales respond boldly to very different values current in Westminster where proposed changes to mental health legislation are predicated on exaggerated concerns about 'public protection'. The proposed reform of the *Mental Health Act* has provoked a storm of opposition uniting almost the entire spectrum of groups involved in mental health, from radical user groups to the Royal College of Psychiatrists.

The proposals, which include a widening of definitions of mental health and an increase in powers of compulsion, are arguably discriminatory and a violation of the right to privacy. They have strong Home Office backing; health legislation is being warped by an agenda focusing increasingly on criminal justice issues and an exaggerated public perception of risk. Although, incidentally, due to changing case law same-sex partners will have to be recognised as nearest relative for those prohibited from leaving hospital on a compulsory section.

To its credit, the Assembly consulted widely on the implications of this legislation for Wales and conveyed strong misgivings to the Minister for Health in Westminster. This may have contributed to the proposed reforms being sent back for redrafting. The proposed reform of the *Mental Health Act* runs directly counter to many aspects of the All Wales *Mental Health Strategy* (2001), a dichotomy that has prompted the Assembly Government to begin to explore the extent of its powers to influence the implementation of primary legislation.

Whether the Assembly is committed and coherent enough in its strategic planning to deliver on visionary statements remains to be seen and the indicators are mixed. With regard to the *Mental Health Strategy* (2001) the haziness around targets, timetables and clear consequences for failure to deliver may not auger well and the lack of resourcing has already become a source of disillusionment to users and service providers. With regard to partnership working, paper partnerships proliferate at local and national level, but too often may not function to achieve real change.

On the one hand, this could be a process of real learning – and the appointment of skilled secondees to advise on the implementation of the strategy is an indication of a wish to listen and learn. On the other hand, there are moves to 'internalise' auditing of health and social services' bodies to Wales, which some commentators worry may ease the pressure produced by unfavourable comparisons with services across the border and lead to complacency.

Overall, as a young institution, the Assembly has proven its ability to develop a vision of its own for mental health services, a vision distinct from that current in the British Parliament. The Assembly has also sought to develop a vision of partnership, working at a local and national level, with attempts to involve stakeholders in the development and implementation of plans. *Building Stronger Bridges*, focusing on partnership with the Voluntary Sector, is the latest example.

The Assembly in its second term will either prove that it has the capacity to deliver on its strategic vision, or it will become more adept at substituting spin for real change. For the people whose experience of mental health services is patchy and often poor, change remains long overdue and 'Cinderella' status seems to be, for the time being, assured.

Time for a change of hats. Donning my cavalier cowboy headgear, it is fair to say that the Assembly has shown a genuine and pro-active willingness to develop the LGB agenda in Wales. For the first time in the UK, a government has shown willing to sponsor a forum for lesbian and gay people, bringing together the work of a multitude of grass roots voluntary services and activists with the need for advocacy and consultation on an all-Wales basis. Sourced from the Promoting Equality Fund, the commitment to the Forum underlines an ability to address the needs of a less popularly recognised minority and I hope will act as a guiding light to governments not only close to home but globally.

One fine example of the Assembly's willingness to follow through its commitment to the lesbian and gay community to further affect integration was the production of the Curriculum and Qualifications Guidance Circular *Sex and Relationships in Schools*

(2002). It firmly addresses the mythology surrounding clause 28 and resulting misconceived fears to address same-sex relationship issues in the classroom – another UK 'first'. Just look at this paragraph of affirmation under the heading 'Sexual identity and sexual orientation':

> It is up to schools to make sure that the needs of all pupils are met in their programmes. Young people need to feel that sex and relationships programmes are relevant to them and sensitive to their needs. They might also find it difficult to talk to their parents or carers about matters of sexuality or sexual orientation. The National Assembly is clear that teachers should be able to deal with these issues honestly, sensitively and in a non-discriminatory way. They should be able to answer appropriate questions and provide factual information. It is important that young people develop an understanding and respect for others regardless of their developing sexual orientation. They should be encouraged to respect and recognise diversity and differences in human life. Section 28 of the Local Government Act 1988 does not prevent the objective discussion of homosexuality in the classroom, and schools can provide counselling, guidance and support for the pupils.

Following paragraphs endorse the above with a call for 'a strong anti-bullying stance' and draw attention to the emotional distress and harm caused by bullying 'related to sexual orientation or for any other reason.'

The achievement of the Assembly in forging a unique path for mental health strategy in Wales could act as precedent for the promotion and adoption of greater civil rights for minority groups elsewhere in the UK. The Assembly has yet to fully test the parameters of its influence and could have a distinctive voice for human rights, for example in backing the promotion of civil registration to the same legal standing as heterosexual marriage.

One factor conducive to the National Assembly's understanding of the needs of minority groups is the accessibility of the Equal Opportunities Committee. The Committee has worked closely with the LGB forum, as it has with the gamut of minority representation networks. It's recent attention to the needs of Wales' gypsy traveller communities, member visits to sites and interviews with gypsy traveller children of different ages and backgrounds shows a genuine desire to listen and 'get it right' for those children, whose future opportunities depend largely on the availability of choice in education and career guidance. The Equal Opportunities Committee's willingness to engage and demonstrable commitment to working with the voluntary sector could be well heeded elsewhere in Assembly partnership structures; consistent Assembly Member presence at regional committees would be a good place to start.

I think it's useful to compare the extent of the Assembly's influence and ability to achieve real change in the two areas of mental health and LGB rights. What shines through is its commitment to the underlying principles of equality of opportunity and social inclusion, in particular in its vision, overall strategy and educative capacity.

Perhaps the challenge it has yet to address is the potential to influence beyond its immediate remit at the complimentary levels of service delivery and legislative change. If they can do that, then I'll take my hats off to them.

Eleanor White co-founded Mind Out Cymru and Mind Works and is currently Amnesty International's Development Officer in Wales.

The National Assembly and International Issues

By Keith Roberts
Head of Oxfam Cymru

It seems a long time since a colleague of mine based at Oxfam GB's Head Office in Oxford said to me: "But you won't be able to do anything with the Welsh Assembly. They won't be interested as there are no devolved powers related to Foreign Affairs or International issues" From the beginning of the National Assembly's life the view of the Oxfam Cymru team was, and continues to be, much more positive. Real opportunities have been given to us by political devolution. This positive attitude is also shared by many of the partner International Non Government Organisation's (NGO's) that we work with in Wales.

Initially in 1999 our view was that there would be numerous opportunities to work with individual National Assembly Members and with the parties in the National Assembly in informal ways. We also believed that there would be potential for developing more [semi] formal ways of working with the National Assembly as it developed as an institution. These beliefs have been strengthened as a result of progress made during the first term of the National Assembly's life.

The reason for our initial confidence that the National Assembly would have potential for various levels of engagement with global and international issues wasn't based on formally devolved powers but on the following framework:

- The long and proud history of internationalism and solidarity as a part of civil society in Wales
- The expressed desire of senior politicians elected to the National Assembly that the developing Wales would be 'externally focused and growing in confidence'
- The requirements of the National Assembly's *Sustainable Development Scheme* and the decision that this would have a cross cutting and Assembly wide remit. [Clearly sustainable development can only be developed thoroughly in a global context]
- The social inclusion, equal opportunities, and partnerships cross cutting agendas of the National Assembly. These can all be informed and strengthened by the experience and perspective of agencies within our sector in Wales that work with these issues on a global scale
- All of the above, in the context of Section 33 of the *Government of Wales Act 1998* which states that : 'The Assembly may consider, and make appropriate representations about any matter affecting Wales'

Our view, shared by numerous members of the National Assembly, was and continues to be, that there is the potential for significant benefit for 'the developing Wales' in learning from, as well as contributing towards, a global social justice and human rights agenda.

Within the above framework we were initially encouraged by a number of results. These included:

- The focus of the first National Assembly St. David's Day Debate being on the Jubilee Debt Campaign
- The public commitment of the First Minister to be identified with the campaign to abolish the Voucher Scheme for asylum seekers. He was the most senior Labour Party politician in the UK to do this
- The work of the National Assembly's Equal Opportunities Committee on asylum and justice issues. This was based on an appreciation of some of the global issues that contribute to people seeking asylum
- The commitment of the *Llywydd* (Presiding Officer) to give space for concerns re: global issues to be addressed in National Assembly Plenary sessions
- The support given to the 'Global View' campaign by National Assembly Members of all parties prior to the Westminster General Election of 2001. This was a campaign to ensure that global issues featured as an issue in the Election and involved 30 + organisations.

One of the major benefits that the National Assembly has brought to many organisations and agencies in Wales is that of accessibility. This has been true for us as well and has shown itself in a variety of ways. The major ones have included the following:

Together with colleagues from CAFOD, Christian Aid, Save the Children, and the Welsh Centre for International Affairs we explored the possibility of the National Assembly setting up an All Party Group on International Development (APGID). This group has now met on a number of occasions with all party representation and has explored numerous issues including Afghanistan, Globalisation and Trade Issues. At our most recent meeting we were encouraged by the Deputy First Minister to identify a number of actions and commitments that we wanted the National Assembly to consider regarding Trade Justice, Sustainable Development and associated issues.

The First Minister is scheduled to speak at our next meeting on the Network of Regional Government for Sustainable Development. [NRG for SD]. This is a very interesting and significant initiative in which the First Minister has exercised a major leadership role. It includes Regional Governments from the North and from the South, [See below] We see this as an area in which APGID can make a distinctive contribution in partnership with the Welsh Assembly Government.

During the 2002 World Summit on Sustainable Development in Johannesburg the First Minister was the prime mover in bringing together this network. This network includes, at present, 23 regional governments including a number from the South. We believe that this initiative places the 'external Wales' agenda very clearly and formally on the agenda of the National Assembly. There are various commitments and aspirations set out in the initial 'Gauteng Declaration' that indicate this. These include:

'...assistance in the development of co-operative projects and programmes between regional governments in different parts of the world to implement Agenda 21, the Johannesburg Plan of Action, and the Millennium Development Targets'

For us as an International NGO committed to finding effective, sustainable and lasting solutions to poverty this will potentially strengthen our working relationship with the National Assembly. This network will inevitably facilitate *Local to Global Learning'* as well as ensuring that voices of people in the South are heard by regional and national governments in the North.

Founder members of the NRG for SD believe that:

It is important that the network should reach out beyond ministers and officials of the regional governments, and should also engage the interest and participation of other stakeholders interested in the promotion of sustainable development at regional level, including the academic community, the business community and NGO's.

If these aspirations and intentions are delivered on they will undoubtedly contribute to "...making globalisation work for sustainable development"...and we would add strongly '...and also for the poor'

The most obvious example of working with the National Assembly that Oxfam has had was the *Cymru a'r Byd'* (Wales and the World) Conference. In April 2002 together with WWF Cymru and the National Assembly we hosted a Wales wide conference with a sustainable development focus.

A wide range of environmental and development issues were addressed by over 400 people from various parts of Wales. Issues such as Education for Sustainable Development, Gender Budgeting, Participation, and Globalisation / Trade Justice were explored. The Conference feedback contributed to the messages that the First Minister took to the Johannesburg Summit a few months later.

A further development from this was that during the First Minister's time at the Johannesburg Summit he spent time with a township community at the Eco City as well as meeting with a leading South African Civil Rights lawyer who is a key player in the HIV Aids Treatment Action Campaign in Southern Africa. It was impressive that in both contexts the First Minister of the Welsh Assembly Government was joining in solidarity with people who had been marginalised in South Africa in ways that meant something to them.

This level of solidarity with people in poverty in the developing world has been expressed in a variety of ways during the first 4 years of the National Assembly's life. It is an essential aspect of Wales being externally focused. We look forward to working with the National Assembly as well as with Welsh civil society, and partner NGO's to ensure that this external engagement is consolidated strategically in the future.

Another significant way in which the National Assembly has enabled us to bring our agenda to the mainstream of its' life has been through its' Voluntary Sector Scheme. Two dimensions of the Scheme have particularly contributed to this.

Firstly, through the establishment of the National Assembly's Voluntary Sector Partnership Council (VSPC). The International Development and Humanitarian Aid sector has a seat on the VSPC. This has helped us in three particular ways in mainstreaming our agenda as follows:

- By having opportunities to make local to global connections in the work of the VSPC. This has happened particularly around issues of Community Building, Partnership Working, Sustainable Development, Participation, and Human Rights. All of these are as relevant to Calcutta as to Cardiff, and to Dar Es Salaam as to Denbigh. There is mutual learning to do.
- By being able to speak on specific issues that are important to our International Development sector. This was particularly true in relation to the Johannesburg Summit. Not surprisingly many of the VSPC members are more than interested in issues of global social justice, human rights, and the development agenda.
- By receiving support from the National Assembly for the development of our network through the Partnership Council Network Support Grant. This has enabled us to strengthen the network, gain broader perspectives, and more effectively fulfil our role within the VSPC.

Secondly through the Ministerial Meetings which take place twice yearly. Together with colleagues from other parts of the Voluntary Sector in Wales we work on the development of strategic agendas for these meetings. We have been involved particularly in meetings with the Education Minister [relating to Education for Sustainable Development] and with the Finance and Communities Minister [relating to the Anti-Poverty Network Cymru, Gender, and Participation agendas].

Interestingly it was also at the first ministerial meeting with the First Minister that we received positive signs of his support for the APGID. Also at this meeting the possibility of his attendance at the Johannesburg Summit was explored.

The people that Oxfam works with on a global scale are people who many Welsh citizens identify with, support, and learn from. Always there is mutual enrichment in such partnership working. The National Assembly and Welsh Assembly Government have already begun to engage in ways that reflect this internationalism and solidarity within the new Political Institution that we now have in Wales.

Let me end with two examples of this.

The first is a human story. It describes a series of informal conversations that took place between Omar, a leader in one of the Coffee Producer Co-operatives in Brazil and Assembly Members. Various National Assembly Members stood and spoke with him in the milling area at Cardiff Bay. One of these conversations was with the First Minister. They engaged in conversation about the hope that in the November Brazilian General Election Lula, the 'Worker Politician' would be elected as President. The level of solidarity and strength could be seen as the conversation progressed.

Omar spent a few weeks in the UK travelling around, meeting many people and giving many talks. But for him, as he completed his post – tour report it was the visit to the National Assembly and the conversations, not only, but particularly, with the First Minister that was his highlight. In Cardiff Bay he experienced solidarity.

The second will have impact on many people, but its' focus is on the forthcoming National Assembly Election in May 2003. Together with a number of other groups and organisations we have produced a document that encourages and challenges the parties and the candidates to take on board specific issues of global and domestic social justice and human rights. These are issues that Assembly Members and the Welsh Assembly Government can make a positive contribution to during the next term of the National Assembly's development. As Civic Nationhood develops in Wales, our hope is that it grows with an 'outward looking face'. Our belief is that the National Assembly can make a most positive and developing contribution to this being delivered.

Keith Roberts has worked for Oxfam GB for five years and is currently Head of Oxfam Cymru. Prior to this he worked for two other UK charities. From 76-91 he was a clergyperson working in two inner-city parishes in London. In both he was involved in community building. He is a member of the National Assembly for Wales VSPC, the WSDF and the Board of the WCVA.

Educating Global Citizens for a Sustainable World!

By Catherine Hester

Curriculum Adviser, Oxfam Cymru and Chair of Cyfanfyd

Devolution in Wales has brought with it a new political climate for debate about Welsh identity, about the nature of citizenship, and about Wales' place in the world. Debate and divided opinion is plentiful around the impact of globalisation, on how best to combat terrorism, on climate change and global warming, or on strategies for developing a prosperous economy in Wales. This is fertile ground for developing a sense of global citizenship – for exploring our responsibilities not only to national priorities, but for taking full account for our impact beyond our own horizons. Global citizenship provides a framework for encouraging exploration of these issues from early years to adult education, and the secondary legislative powers on education policy have meant that Wales can find its own way to raise the profile of these issues.

Within Wales, there has been a general acceptance of the term " Global Citizenship" to describe education with a global perspective. Oxfam defines a global citizen as someone who:

- Is aware of the wider world and has a sense of their own role as a world citizen
- Respects and values diversity
- Is willing to act to make the world a more equitable and sustainable place
- Takes responsibility for their actions
- Is outraged by social injustice
- Participates in and contributes to the community at a range of levels from the local to the global
- Has an understanding of how the world works economically, politically, socially, culturally, technologically and environmentally.

Global citizenship is about developing specific ways of thinking, feeling and behaving: it is about taking responsibility for our lives, our relationships, and our impact on others. Children spend a great deal of their time in a formal education setting – consciously acquiring knowledge and skills, and unconsciously shaping their values and attitudes about the world around them. The classroom is a perfect breeding ground for curious beings, who recognise that there is a big world beyond their own horizons, a world that regularly touches their own lives in a number of ways and who realise that they can make a difference to that world.

In 1995, Cyfanfyd, or 'whole world' was formally constituted as the Development Education Association in Wales – working to promote global citizenship in all sectors. The many diverse organisations working here needed a strategic advocacy voice that would represent their views, and promote good practice amongst the membership. The organisation has strong links with sister organisations across the UK, and through this with networks across Europe.

Membership of Cyfanfyd is diverse, including the main development NGOs, such as Oxfam Cymru, Christian Aid, CAFOD, Save The Children and UNICEF, Development Education Centres, CEWC Cymru, multicultural arts organisations, and a number of higher education colleges. Our contacts in Higher Education (HE) are mainly with Initial Teacher Education and Training (ITET) establishments, adult and continuing education departments and departments specialising in development issues. Cyfanfyd promotes global citizenship in three sectors – youth work, life-long learning and formal education.

With increasingly significant opportunities to work with and to influence the Welsh Assembly Government in terms of education policy, and with the additional strategic framework for development awareness being developed by Department for International Development (DfID), critical opportunities arose for Cyfanfyd to move from being a small voice for issues many saw as far from mainstream, to becoming a credible partner is shaping policy in practice, building on the integrity of its membership. It is fair to say that this transition from protagonist to partner has brought with it a steep learning curve, and a need to relinquish natural scepticisms on both sides.

Education, previously the remit of the Welsh Office, has now become the responsibility of the National Assembly. As a result of this, Cyfanfyd has been able to engage directly in shaping the development of education policy in Wales, through both formal and informal consultation and dialogue. Examples of this engagement include the developments of the Curriculum 2000 and the Personal and Social Education (PSE) Framework, as Cyfanfyd channelled the views of its membership in to these debates. As the Assembly has increasingly incorporated global citizenship and sustainable development in to its education policy work, a number of opportunities have arisen to address the Education and Lifelong Learning Committee. These opportunities to engage directly with Assembly Members involved with education has reiterated the widespread support for, and commitment to these issues across all political boundaries.

In 2002, Cyfanfyd was a significant supporting partner in developing the booklet *Education for Sustainable Development and Global Citizenship* (ESDGC). This publication, sponsored by the Assembly, Estyn, ACCAC and DFID, is a first formal step at highlighting the potential for delivering ESDGC in schools. Cyfanfyd was instrumental in shaping content, and providing case studies for the booklet. In 2003 Cyfanfyd will again provide strategic support directly to the Assembly in assisting the development of a follow-up document *Global Citizenship: a Guide for Curriculum Planners*.

> Young people today are growing up in a world where prosperity and technological progress exist alongside mass poverty and an environment under threat…Education for sustainable development and global citizenship is not an extra subject of study. It is a way of approaching the existing school curriculum and school life. It can be liberating for learners and teachers alike.
>
> Jane Davidson, Minister for Education and Life-long Learning
> (*Education for Sustainable Development and Global Citizenship* booklet, Nov. 2002)

Currently Cyfanfyd has three distinct channels for regularly engaging in debate on policy and practice with the Assembly. These channels are used to ensure that a coherent approach to promoting both global citizenship and sustainable development is adopted by the Assembly and by statutory bodies in Wales.

Ministerial Meetings - The bi-annual Ministerial meetings are organised by Welsh Council for Voluntary Action, as part of the Assembly's commitment to liaise formally with representatives of the Voluntary Sector. In 2000, Cyfanfyd used this channel to lobbying for the establishment of an advisory panel on education for sustainable development (APESD).

Advisory Panel on Education for Sustainable Development - This body has currently been in operation for about two years, and Cyfanfyd's representation on APESD has ensured that social and economic factors, as well as environmental, are at the heart of the Assembly's understanding of ESD. Projects have been funded to develop models of good practice for ESD in schools, for developing a 'who's who' directory of service providers in Wales, and for a training of trainers workshop. Research has also been conducted in to Initial Teacher Education and Training (ITET) in Wales, to elicit current levels of good practice and determine appropriate future steps to help the colleges to embed global citizenship and sustainable development in to ITET.

Working Group on Global Citizenship - In 1997 the DfID published a white paper called *Building Support for Development*. One of the many commitments contained within this was a call for 'development awareness to form part of an entitlement curriculum for all children in the UK'. In order to progress this, a 'Working Group on Global Citizenship' was established as a partnership between the DfID and the Assembly, with representation from key strategic partners, including Cyfanfyd.

Further opportunities for influence have been presented by some of the key policies of the Assembly. The Assembly has a statutory duty under the *Government of Wales Act 1998* to promote sustainable development in the exercise of its function. The development and process of consulting on the Assembly's scheme for sustainable development, has enabled development and environmental education organisations in Wales to lobby for a strong position for Education for Sustainable Development. More scope to engage in the public debate has also been provided by the Assembly's commitment to social inclusion and equal opportunities as expressed in *the Better Wales* policy document, the Assembly's ten year plan to improve life in Wales.

The Assembly's 'Extending Entitlement' Model for the informal education of young people highlights the need for informal and formal education structures to be streamlined. This has provided a unique opportunity to incorporate global citizenship and sustainable development into all aspects of youth work in Wales. Cyfanfyd is playing a strategic role in supporting this through its successful application to the DfID Development Awareness fund for a Global Youth Work development officer. The GYW development officer is based at the Wales Youth Agency, and is tasked with influencing training and education policy through the inclusion of development awareness in the youth work curriculum statement and training programmes. This model of partnership between a Development Education network and a statutory youth work body is unique within the UK.

The life long learning sector also provides strategic opportunities for engaging with global citizenship, as well as the Assembly's strategic priorities of social inclusion, equal opportunities and sustainable development. Cyfanfyd has developed a strategic partnership with Worker's Education Association (WEA) South Wales to 'globalise' the curriculum through providing in-service training for tutors and outreach workers. We hope that in future the Assembly will support further initiatives to develop this – ensuring that global citizenship and sustainable development are embedded within adult and youth work, as well as formal education.

Devolution has enabled the Assembly to begin creating an education system that is specifically targeted at the needs and aspirations of young people in Wales. It has led to the development of distinct policies and partnerships that are not evident in England. A concrete example of this is the Working Group on Global Citizenship (WGGC), the first formalised collaboration between Ministers within the Assembly and DFID. Whilst the Assembly has responsibility for all matters of education and training, DFID has a UK-wide remit with regard to 'development awareness' among young people. The WGGC has facilitated collaboration between all the agencies involved in this area, including Cyfanfyd, and provided a focus for sharing of good practice between the voluntary sector and the statutory education bodies.

The Education and Life-long Learning Committee, guided by the Minister, Jane Davidson, has demonstrated the capacity and willingness to foster an education system that engages proactively with global citizenship. In partnership with the voluntary sector, we can create a framework for encouraging young people to be active global citizens of Wales and of the world.

Catherine Hester is an experienced primary teacher and special needs worker. She currently works for Oxfam Cymru as Curriculum Adviser, a post she has held for four years. Catherine joined Oxfam after returning from two years with VSO in Tanzania, where she ran a non-formal education programme for street children. She is responsible for the delivery of Oxfam's Development Education programme across Wales, looking at how to integrate global citizenship and sustainable development in to all aspects of the formal education system. For the past two years Catherine has also been Chair of Cyfanfyd, the Development Education Association in Wales.

The Rights of a Child in Wales

By Catriona Williams

Chief Executive Children in Wales

Following ratification of the *UN Convention on the Rights of the Child* (UNCRC), the UK Government is required to prepare a report every four years on the progress it has made in implementing the Convention. The UNCRC is recognised world-wide as the minimum set of standards by which countries can measure their progress.

In the Autumn of 2002, the UNCRC prepared its response to the UK Government's second report and contained within its text was welcome recognition of the significant progress made in Wales. Whilst acknowledgement was also given to a variety of areas of work in other jurisdictions in the UK, particularly strong praise was reserved for Wales in relation to major key aspects of policy development and implementation that the Committee regard as fundamental to improving the lives of children and young people. The appointment of an independent statutory Children's Commissioner was recognised as the major mechanism by which the implementation of the UNCRC can be monitored on behalf of children and the *National Strategy* based on the principles of the UNCRC were commended by the Committee as significant and important developments.

Since devolution, the Welsh Assembly Government has shown a commitment to introducing the UNCRC into its policy documents relating to children and young people. The *Strategy for Children and Young People* states that the Convention 'should provide the foundation of principle for all dealings with children.' The Welsh Assembly Government has also established a Cabinet Children's Committee that brings together the First Minister, Minister for Health and Social Services, Minister for Education and Lifelong Learning and the Minister for Culture and Sport. Other structures that allow children and young people to express their views such as '*Funky Dragon*', the Children and Young People's Assembly for Wales and the policy initiatives designed to improve children's participation at local level with the requirement for every local authority to establish a youth forum and every school to establish a school council are also pioneering. More recently, the policy initiatives aimed at ensuring the participation of children and young people in the work of local partnerships also provide the foundations upon which to build future policies. Wales is now one of the front-runners in Europe in relation to its policies on the participation of children and young people in policy development. It is however far too early to tell whether these policy initiatives will actually achieve the desired beneficial outcomes for children themselves in their everyday lives.

Another important UK precedent in relation to young people was contained within the *Youth Support Directions (Wales) 2002* whereby local authorities are required to provide youth support services; secure the provision of youth support services or participate in the provision of youth support services. This requirement laid the foundations to redress the previously diminishing youth services where provision was discretionary.

When the Labour Government was elected in Westminster, it was hoped that the opportunity for policy making to be brought nearer to children, young people and their families in Wales would materialise through the process of devolution. Historically, policies relating to children had emanated from issues and practice in London, Birmingham and other large metropolitan centres. Invariably, these policies had not transferred easily into the Welsh situation. The uniqueness of the south Wales valleys communities, with the widespread unemployment resulting from closure of the coal mines, plus vast rural areas and the lack of huge inner city conurbation's, had presented a conflict for those developing policies for children in Wales. Making policies that had originated outside of Wales fit the Welsh situation was like trying 'to squeeze square pegs into round holes'.

One particularly important issue for policy development and implementation in Wales was the detrimental impact on children of the effects of poverty on their health and well-being. Of course this was later formally acknowledged when much of Wales acquired the status of a European Objective One area, thus officially confirming that it is one of the poorest regions in the whole of Europe and consequently warranting extra targeted funding to combat social exclusion. It had long caused concern that key issues were not being identified from the Welsh situation, particularly the effects of poverty. The GDP per head of population is 82% of the UK average. In this context, definitions such as 'children in need' under the *Children Act 1989* for example, had been particularly challenging for some local authorities where there were whole communities whose children suffered the adverse effects of poverty.

The *Government of Wales Act 1998*, that created the National Assembly for Wales, was a radical improvement in terms of the opportunity to make policy that was relevant to the particular needs of Wales. Children in Wales had already been active in supporting the All Party Parliamentary Group of MP's for children in Wales in Westminster and as such had had experience of lobbying for amendments to legislation. Indeed, we had generated debates in parliament about establishing a Children's Commissioner for Wales during the passage of the Bills to re organise local government and also to establish the Assembly.

Devolution created a welcome all Wales opportunity in respect of many matters, but also a complicated and disconnected policy framework between Wales and England. Whilst most matters concerning children and young people are devolved, there are still significant non-devolved responsibilities such as youth justice that remain within the Home Office remit.

The challenge for us in the children's field was how to win over the new Assembly to create structures that would promote implementation of the UNCRC across all aspects of children's lives.

In Wales, the climate was right for a focus on children's rights, as the Welsh Office had already appointed a Minister for Children who was very interested in creating a Children's Commissioner for Wales. There was also interest in such a development from the newly elected Assembly politicians who had a rights based philosophy.

Not long into their first term, the Assembly had to deal with the report of the Waterhouse 'Lost in Care' Tribunal of Inquiry into the Abuse of Children in Public Care in North Wales (1999) that had originally been instigated by the previous Conservative administration. The Tribunal's findings were presented to the Westminster Parliament on 15 February 2000. This was the single largest inquiry to have been undertaken in Wales. The 72 recommendations encompassed the broad range of a child's experience of the public care system. Notably they included 'the appointment of an Independent Children's Commissioner for Wales'. This had however been no coincidence as the Tribunal had received many submissions from key players in the children's field recommending this course of action.

The fact that the political balance of the Assembly resulted in a coalition government with 7 of the Cabinet from Labour and one from the Liberal Democrats, was a very useful development because the workings of the Assembly tended to be much less adversarial than those of the Westminster.

Consensus around issues relating to children and young people was in fact achieved relatively easily, although the key was to adequately brief organisations making responses to the Assembly when it consulted on the issue. The working methods of the Welsh Assembly Government were also conducive to the involvement of outside bodies in the development of policies. The fact that Committees invite organisations in to give presentations and to discuss policy issues and the ethos of the Welsh Assembly Government institution of openness and inclusiveness, with unprecedented accessibility of documentation on the official web site, enabled organisations to keep in touch with developments and to intervene where appropriate. Accessibility of Assembly Members and Ministers to those involved in working with children and young people and also to children and young people themselves was particularly important in creating the dialogue that lead to the establishment of the first Children's Commissioner in the UK.

Having been involved in a UK wide campaign since 1991, Children in Wales coordinated the Children's Commissioner Campaign Group in Wales that included representatives from statutory and voluntary organisations. Through prior European and International work we were familiar with the role of Commissioners and Ombudsmen in a variety of countries and had in the previous few years brought a range of them to speak at our conferences in Wales and to meet politicians.

There were many arguments for establishing the Children's Commissioner in order to address some of the shortcomings in the arrangements for children's services. The UN Committee on the Rights of the Child, had explicitly recommended the creation of an 'Ombudsman' or 'Commissioner' as a means of ensuring children's rights are promoted more effectively. In other words there was no formal mechanism to ensure implementation of the UNCRC in Wales. There was also the fact that children didn't have the vote nor could they influence through powerful lobbies and institutions that inform social and political change so this meant that their views were not incorporated into the development of policies although they were users of a wide range of services. In addition, the fact that benefits from investing in services for children do not become apparent until the child grows up and as a result, had generally meant that investing in children tended to be outweighed by shorter term economic considerations was another key issue.

Waterhouse had clearly shown that children were particularly vulnerable to ill treatment by those more powerful than they are and however proactive voluntary organisations were in highlighting the views of children, they could only influence from outside and had no rights to have their views heard. The North Wales Tribunal had only come into being after a considerable amount of time and public outcry, whereas had there been a mechanism through the office of a Children's Commissioner, the matters could have been raised authoritatively and earlier action could have been taken with considerably less expense.

In Wales and the UK as a whole, there was no explicit recognition of children's civil and political rights so this weakened the position of children seeking redress of violations of rights and diminished the likelihood of formal channels for so doing.

Another argument was the fact that responsibility for services for children was split between the Assembly and other government departments such as the Home Office and within the Assembly between subject committees. The issue of poor communication or collaboration between and within departments with a resultant failure to develop integrated services and no overview of their impact on children themselves needed addressing. Furthermore, in those service areas not directly providing for children, but which impact on them, such as transport policy, environmental health or housing, there was often little consideration at all of the implications of policy for children's lives.

There were many examples of legislation and systems where little attention was paid to the UN Convention on the Rights of the Child, such as within the education system. Children did not have access to advocacy or complaints procedures in a wide range of services such as health and not all services had formal inspectorates. Finally, large numbers of children were not only vulnerable as a result of simply being children, but also due to their membership of other groups who experience marginalisation, stigma and discrimination. Such groups included refugees, travellers, children with disabilities, homeless children, those in poverty, children "looked after", members of minority ethnic communities, children in prison and children living with violence. These children faced double or multiple jeopardy and were extremely vulnerable to exploitation by and exclusion from the society in which they live.

The Assembly approached the task of considering the value of establishing such an office through a lengthy consultation period following an initial briefing from Children in Wales. A wide range of organisations gave oral as well as written evidence and the end product was a report from the Assembly that met with approval from the campaigners and had the unanimous vote of the Assembly. A particular feature of the report was recognition that the Commissioner should have powers over non-devolved as well as devolved matters.

As the first Wales specific legislation since devolution, it was introduced as an amendment to the *Care Standards Bill 2000* before the self-standing *Children's Commissioner Bill for Wales* that extended the powers to 'any matter affecting the rights and welfare of children in Wales' was introduced the following parliamentary session and was passed was the *Children's Commissioner for Wales Act 2001*. It was during this process that it became apparent that the original aspirations of the Assembly, were being curtailed by the government departments that had jurisdiction over non-devolved matters. Whilst in line with the devolution settlement, from a child's perspective and therefore from the Children in Wales Campaign Group's perspective, it was unsatisfactory to have a Children's Commissioner with powers over most aspects of their lives, but not over those legislated for by Whitehall Departments. Further intensive lobbying was undertaken including a meeting with the Attorney General in order to encourage an amendment to the Bill. In fact this was successful in part because the government was persuaded to introduce an amendment that at least allowed the Commissioner to make comment about non-devolved matters to the Assembly. It did however fall well short of the powers the role had in relation to devolved matters. A future challenge for the Welsh Assembly Government is to ensure that MP's from Wales, particularly those in the Wales Office who represent the Assembly's interests in Whitehall, are fully in tune with the ethos of the rights based approach adopted by the Assembly.

A significant aspect of the way in which the legislation was handled related to reference to the UNCRC itself. Whilst reference to the UNCRC in primary legislation had been rejected, the Assembly included it in the secondary legislation, again indicating a stronger commitment to the UNCRC in Wales.

A second major development regarding implementation of the UNCRC in Wales is in relation to the abolition of the defence of reasonable chastisement in the case of children. Following a concerted campaign across the UK from children's organisations, the Welsh Assembly Government was the first to legislate through the *Childminding and Day Care (Wales) Regulations 2002* that came into force on 1st April 2002. The result is that there is secondary legislation in Wales prohibiting the physical chastisement by childminders of children in their care and this is not the case anywhere else in the UK. In our view, the full extent of the potential of other secondary legislation has not yet been realised.

In order to positively change children's lives, adequate and appropriately targeted resources are needed. In order to assess need, good quality information is required. The Welsh Assembly Government published a statistical focus on Children in Wales in November 2002, which is a start in that it becomes clear where the crucial gaps in relation to data exist. The population of Wales is around 3 million, and roughly 20% are children under 18 years of age. There has been an ongoing problem regarding the appropriate disaggregation of data on a Wales and a UK basis. This became particularly apparent when the UK government sent its report to the UN. The UN Committee recommended that there should be 'an analysis of all sectoral and total budgets and in the devolved administrations in order to show the percentage spent on children, identify priorities and allocate resources to the 'maximum extent of available resources'.

If this information is available and acted upon; if the independent Children's Commissioner acts as an appropriate watchdog; and if the UNCRC is implemented in accordance with the Welsh Assembly Government's current policy direction; Wales' children may have a brighter future than had devolution not happened at all. However, policy documents and legislative successes are only the start and the Assembly will be judged on its long term effect on the health and well being of its children and young people.

Catriona Williams has been the Chief Executive of Children in Wales since 1991 and as well as Wales and UK based activity, she is President of the European Forum for Child Welfare and a member of the Executive Committee of the International Forum for Child Welfare. Children in Wales is the National Umbrella membership body in Wales for organisations and individuals working with and for children and young people with a broad based membership drawn from all disciplines and sectors.

Adjusting to Adversity

By Ann Jones

Labour Assembly Member for Vale of Clwyd
Team Wales and The Children's Society

There can be no question that recent years have seen children's issues pushed up the political agenda in Wales. This has also been the case in the rest of Britain, but a combination of devolution and previous developments, specifically the uncovering of the widespread abuse which took place in north Wales during the 1970's and 1980's led to a particular spotlight being placed on child protection in Wales. One of the key breakdowns highlighted by Sir Ronald Waterhouse was the way in which the complaints and concerns expressed by some of the abused children failed to be heeded at the time. The *Waterhouse Report* (1999) underlined the importance of high quality, independent advocacy services for vulnerable children and young people. By 2001, The Children's Society was running a dozen advocacy projects across Wales, with most of their funding coming from the relevant local authorities in what was seen as an excellent example of partnership working between statutory authorities and the voluntary sector.

Then on 6 November 2001 came a bolt from the blue. The Children's Society announced that, due to financial difficulties, it was to cut 20% of its services in England and withdraw completely from all its work in Wales. The decision had been taken by the Trustees in London a fortnight previously. There was no attempt at advance consultation with the Assembly, local authority partners or even with representatives of their own staff in Wales.

Needless to say the announcement aroused a storm of protest. The then Archbishop of Wales, Dr Rowan Williams, resigned as Honorary Vice President of the society. I myself led a debate in the Assembly which saw all four parties united in condemnation of the decision and the manner in which it had been reached. Welsh Health and Social Services Minister Jane Hutt summoned the Society's management to explain their position and announced that she was setting up a special taskforce, to examine whether, and if so how, the services that were being provided by The Children's Society could be preserved. As temporary Chair of the Health and Social Services Committee, during my colleague Kirsty Williams AM's absence on maternity leave, I was invited to join the taskforce in order to lend extra political weight to its work. The taskforce was co-ordinated by Children in Wales, an umbrella organisation that represents and advises the various voluntary groups who work with children in the principality.

I wish I could say that The Children's Society was co-operative in its work with the taskforce. It did not hinder us, and claimed to be fully supportive of our objectives, but its primary concern seemed to be the protection of it's reserves against any request for a share to be given over in order to provide launch funding for a Welsh successor. Their main focus was to cut their liabilities in Wales, as they perceived them, and withdraw as rapidly as possible.

Despite this stance, we did secure some funding from the Society. The legal position in relation to the legacies and other funds which came to them from Wales was critical to these negotiations. The Assembly Government made a significant contribution, and several local authorities, despite having been badly burned, were very understanding and happy to assist our efforts to preserve the services more or less intact.

In August 2002 we saw the launch of a new body, Tros Gynnal; it has taken over most of the projects and is receiving support from Children in Wales. One previous project had been taken over by the Church in Wales. I very much hope that Tros Gynnal will clearly show that we in Wales do not simply whine about the shameful way we are sometimes treated, but can shape our own future by responding to such adversity by taking matters into our own hands, finding our own Welsh solutions.

The Children's Society is as 'blue chip' as charities get. Its honorary president is the Archbishop of Canterbury, and patrons, back in 2001, included HM the Queen Mother. Founded in 1881 it was, in effect, the primary domestic philanthropic arm of the Church of England and the Church in Wales.

So how did this mess develop? As the days and weeks drew on, it seemed to me that the excuses proffered by the society grew more and more intricate. One could not help believing that that they were inventing excuses to try and justify a decision taken in haste, without adequate reflection. In an article for the respected social work journal *Community Care* (2001) the Society's Chief Executive, Mr Ian Sparks, alleged that advocacy services had been made a statutory requirement in Wales and that the Welsh Assembly had refused the Society's grant applications. The state of the law in relation to advocacy services in Wales remains the same as in England – (though Mr Sparks might possibly have been confused by the advocacy capacity exercised by the Independent Children's Commissioner for Wales). Also the Children's Society had never in fact made any applications for funding direct to the Assembly. It was later clarified that Mr Sparks had been referring to applications for European Objective One funding, which were turned down because they failed to meet the European Commission's requirements in relation to 'additionality'.

When I showed the *Community Care* article to my colleague Jane Hutt it is fair to say that she hit the roof. The Assembly does have funding streams that could potentially have been accessed in support of the advocacy projects run by the Children's Society. For instance, Section 64 grants or grants through the Children and Youth Partnership Fund. As Jane made clear, partnership is a two way street. If the society had, at an early stage, approached her officials and privately explained the difficulties they faced, it would have been much easier to provide rescue funding at that time than after the Society had effectively pointed a gun at the Assembly by announcing a unilateral decision to close the projects.

Although the society's senior management declined to come and explain their decisions to the Assembly, they did not risk contempt of Parliament by refusing to give evidence to the Welsh Affairs Select Committee (WASC). If any proof is needed of the continuing worth of WASC following the establishment of the Assembly, this is surely it.

The Select Committee cross-examined the Chief Executive and Finance Director. Also called before it were the Chair of the Board of Trustees and the only Welsh Trustee, my own local vicar, the Revd John Glover, who had first alerted me to the crisis and who had been the sole member of the 23 strong Board of Trustees to vote against the proposal. Only a few months beforehand, in July 2001, John had become the Chair of a Welsh Advisory Committee set up by the Society following a detailed study of the impact of devolution and Welsh identities on their operations in Wales. I know that, at that time, John felt that the Society's operations in Wales were being put on a solid footing. He was devastated to be confronted just two months down the line with a recommendation that the Society should pull out and had been on the brink of resigning from the Board in protest, though I and others eventually persuaded him that he could do more good by remaining. The other three witnesses faced a robust cross-examination, which I travelled to London to observe.

As the Select Committee teased out the facts it became clear that the decision making process of the Board had been seriously flawed and concluded that the Board had been wrongly informed as to the status of the projects and the agreements with certain of the local authorities. The Chair of the Board, Lady Toulson confirmed that that was the first ever meeting she had attended as a Trustee. It was clear to the Welsh Affairs Committee that the decision had been heavily influenced by the senior management who had closed off information and discussion of alternatives and steered the Board very strongly toward the, in my opinion erroneous, conclusion that there was no alternative but to pull out completely. As they themselves put it (2002):

> The Committee accepts that the Society is facing financial difficulties … however it concludes that the Society is unable to offer compelling reasons for the decision to withdraw entirely from Wales, rather than to implement some other pattern of cuts. It regrets the fact that nobody, not even the Society's own managers in Wales was consulted before the decision was taken and that it appears to have been taken hastily, without the involvement of the Society's own Welsh Advisory Group and on the basis of inaccurate or incomplete information.

At the Committee's request, a copy of their report was sent to the Charities Commission. In their response, the Charities Commissioners described the process by which the trustees took steps to inform themselves as having had 'shortcomings' and the widespread criticism of the failure to consult as 'understandable', going on to note that 'the possibility cannot be excluded that consultation of statutory funders might have generated 'rescue' funding opportunities.' Finally the Commission stated that the Society 'cannot be said to have managed its financial circumstances as successfully in some respects as could, and arguably should, have been the case.' In effect, the Charities Commission confirmed the main criticisms made by the Welsh Affairs Committee. However, the Charities Commission concluded that despite the shortcomings, the Trustees decision could not be proven to be invalid from a legal perspective.

Aside from the devastating impact on the provision of advocacy services for vulnerable children in Wales, there were two other issues of wider relevance which the whole sorry affair highlighted. These relate to the Welsh Language and to the whole future of partnership working between local and national government and the voluntary sector.

A principal justification for withdrawing from Wales was centred on the cost of providing services in Wales. The Society argued that its spending in Wales was considerably greater than the amount of funding raised in Wales, though to this day they continue to raise funds in Wales, for instance a shop in Ruthin, just outside of my own constituency, that support work now carried out in England alone. As they themselves put it 'the reality remains that the Society has been subsidising its work on Wales from donations made in England.' This is the case with most UK wide charities, and indeed with the government. Overall government spending in Wales is substantially greater than the amount we contribute in taxes. The reason is straightforward. Wales GDP is the second lowest in the whole of the UK. Sadly the Children's Society did not take the view that the use of money raised voluntarily in richer areas to fund services in poorer areas is one of their defining purposes – a bizarre position for a charity which once prided itself on its Christian ethos!

Within this overall argument, the Society also pointed out that the cost of Welsh Language provision made service provision in Wales more expensive in absolute terms than the cost of working in England. The Society is not as a charity bound by the *Welsh Language Act,* however in a more enlightened phase, recognising that not having a Welsh Language Scheme contravened the UN Convention on the Rights of a Child, which the Society formally adopted in 1996, they did develop such a scheme in consultation with the Welsh Language Board. At no point did the Society ever raise with the Welsh Language Board any concerns relating to the cost of its policy, and it could have trimmed its Welsh language provision at any time.

Following the Welsh Affairs Committee's criticism, the Charities Commission sought a legal opinion which demonstrated that any organisation or company is free to decide against providing services in Wales by pleading the allegedly burdensome costs of Welsh language requirements. It would be hard to imagine a court entertaining similar pleas in relation to health and safety or non-discrimination legislation. Whatever ones views in respect of the Welsh language, it is clear that this is not a satisfactory situation and that the state of the law thus revealed needs to be taken into account in any debate over extending the scope of the *Welsh Language Act.*

The other issue of wider relevance concerns the lessons to be drawn by the Assembly and by local councils in relation to their future dealings with voluntary organisations. Such bodies can add a great deal of value to the work of government over a huge range of fields. The enthusiasm, skills and dedication of an army of volunteers is a vital resource in Wales, plugging gaps in provision, supplementing and enhancing services provided by the state. The Assembly has been extremely keen to encourage the voluntary sector to extend its role further, recognising the strengths that the sector can bring to the development of leaner, more intelligent services, with a better focus on the needs and individuality of those they serve. The actions of the Children's Society however have forced us all to question just how far any voluntary organisation, however respectable can be relied upon.

The Children's Society themselves seemed blithely unconcerned about the impact that their action might have on sister charities (e.g. the NSPCC, NCH Action for Children, Barnardos etc.) operating across the UK and remaining in Wales. So far as the Children's

Society was concerned, this was none of their business. The rest of the Voluntary Sector saw things somewhat differently. They recognised that it is only on the basis of trust and confidence on both sides that effective partnerships between government and themselves can be made to work. To their credit, most Social Services Directors and other officials whom I have spoken to do not appear to have been so scarred by their experience of being let down by the Children's Society as to let it prejudice their dealings with other voluntary groups. It is however now more clearly recognised among AM's, councillors, and the wider Welsh public that there are limits to the role that voluntary organisations can be entrusted with in the delivery of vital services to the most vulnerable groups in our society.

As a direct consequence of the saga with The Children's Society, the Assembly and the Wales Council for Voluntary Action have now drawn up a code of principles which include an explicit commitment to early and genuine consultation with funders, other stakeholders, and service users in Wales, in advance of any decision to withdraw, or significantly alter services in Wales. We are asking all voluntary bodies which operate in any other country, including other parts of the UK, to sign up to this code of practice, which we intend to make a condition of such bodies receiving any element of public funding. We are also asking the UK government for assistance in enforcing sanctions against signatories who break the principles of this code. I regret that this has had to be done. Before the actions taken by The Children's Society I would not have believed it to be necessary. The Wales Council for Voluntary Action and its member organisations have been very understanding and have worked with us in developing this code, though we all pray it will never have to be applied.

Ann Jones, prior to her election to the Assembly, was a Rhyl Town Councillor and a Denbighshire County Councillor. Born in 1953, Ann has lived all of her life in Rhyl. She spent 29 years working as a fire brigade control room operator and served as a Fire Brigade Union national official. Interests include health, education, tourism, community safety and regeneration, Social Policy and the Emergency Services. She is chair of the Assembly's Equality of Opportunities Committee and member of Health and Social Services Committee and the North Wales Regional Committee.

Just as Iron Sharpens Iron

The Christian Voluntary Sector and The National Assembly for Wales

By Daniel Boucher

Gweini Policy Development Officer and National Assembly Liaison Officer for the Evangelical Alliance

'People learn from one another, just as iron sharpens iron.'

Proverbs 27. 17

'…State and civil society should act in partnership each to facilitate, but also to act as a control upon, the other.'

Anthony Giddens, *The Third Way*, p. 79.

'The vital organisational strength of our churches, chapels, friendship societies and so on is their roots within local communities. It is this strength that makes our church based groups so vital in terms of community regeneration and empowerment the people doing the work come from, and are themselves, members of the community.'

Ann Jones AM, Gweini *Bulletin*

'The "church" makes a massive input into community services of all kinds, offering most aspects of care from early years provision to Day Care, luncheon clubs and support for particularly vulnerable groups in society. But the "church" is also very good at hiding its contribution. '

Janet Ryder AM, Gweini *Bulletin*

Churches have always been involved in welfare provision. Not so long ago there was a real sense in which the churches were the welfare state. With the coming of the *Beveridge Report,* however, the perception was that state provision largely displaced the churches' welfare role (See, Dickey, Brian, 'Going about and doing good', John Wolffe, *Evangelical Faith and Public Zeal*, London, SPCK, 1995. p. 54.) Since then there has of course been a renaissance of voluntarism, especially in the last twenty years, (See Kendall and Knapp, The Voluntary Sector in the United Kingdom, Manchester, Manchester University Press, 1996, p. 139) but the resulting new voluntary sector seems overwhelmingly secular. All this, moreover, has taken place in a context where the container for the Christian Voluntary Sector, the church has experienced significant decline. But what are the actual implications of this decline for the Christian Voluntary Sector and its relationship to the National Assembly?

When you are very big you can fall a long way in proportional terms and still constitute a very significant part of society in absolute terms. In 1851 57% of people regularly attended church or chapel. (See Griffith, WP, Preaching second to no Other under the Sun, Religion and National Identity: Wales and Scotland c 17600-200, Ed Robert Pope, Cardiff, University of Wales Press, 2001, p. 63.) Today the figure is more like 7%. (See Brierley, Peter, *Religious Trends 3, UK Christian Handbook*, 2002/3, p. 2.23.) What a reduction! Having said this, though, 7% of 2.9 million is a lot of people. More people attend church on Sunday than go to football matches on Saturday or who are members of political parties. There are not many civil society institutions that engage with as much as 7% of the population. Furthermore, whilst some denominations have experienced decline, the last eighty years have also witnessed a revolution in Welsh non-conformism giving rise to a series of new denominations that now, along with the Anglicans, Baptists, Presbyterians and other historic denominations, constitute the Welsh church. These denominations including for example the Assemblies of God Church, the Elim Pentecostal Church, the Apostolic Church, Pioneer Churches, Associating Evangelical Churches of Wales (AECW) etc, have in many cases relatively young age profiles and the energy to make a significant welfare contribution. Indeed it is now recognized that churches are a tremendous source of volunteering within society. (See the Local Government Association's, *Faith and Community: A Guide to Best Practice*; 3.5 'Not the least of the reasons why a local authority should consider the relationship with its faith communities is the contribution they make to 'active communities' initiatives. Research by the Institute for Volunteering Research for example indicates that members of churches synagogues and other faith communities are more likely to contribute their free time to helping others.' The Local Government Association, Feb 2001).

Thus, whilst there can be no doubting that church attendance has been falling, this has not placed Christian voluntarism in jeopardy. Although it is true that the new voluntary sector has a largely secular profile, it has not displaced the older Christian Voluntary Sector that preceded both it and the welfare state. The Christian Voluntary Sector endures and is making an important contribution in the twenty-first century through the provision of a diverse range of projects including parent and toddler initiatives, drug rehabilitation units, soup runs, homelessness initiatives, job start programmes, youth exclusion projects, educational projects, youth work, lunch clubs etc.

The most immediate challenge facing the Christian Voluntary Sector as it confronted its relationship with the National Assembly for Wales in 1999 was the general lack of recognition of its reality and significance. 'This had been eloquently demonstrated when in the previous year the Welsh Office drew together a representative grouping of the Voluntary Sector in Wales which did not include any churches or para church bodies (See Welsh Office and Wales Council for Voluntary Action, *Compact between the Government and the Voluntary Sector in Wales*, November 1998, p. 14.) It was almost as if the Christian Voluntary Sector did not exist. Something had to be done.

In this environment there was a clear appreciation that there was a need for a devoted Christian Voluntary Sector umbrella body that could promote the sector in Wales. It was thus in October 1999 that Gweini (the Welsh for 'to serve'): The Council of Christian Community Work in Wales came into being.

Gweini's board, headed by Rev Julian Richards (Director) and Gill Capper JP (President), defined its objectives in terms of two broad activities each of which engaged with the

National Assembly. **Representation:** Gweini was to seek to impact policy development in the National Assembly, responding to consultations, adding value to the policy process and demonstrating the reality of a vibrant Christian Voluntary Sector. **Capacity Building:** Gweini was also to make the Christian Voluntary Sector aware of National Assembly policy and funding developments, helping the sector to fully engage with changes in these areas.

There is more to the funding rationale than one might first presume. In considering the problem of invisibility there was recognition at the time of the formation of Gweini that the Christian Voluntary Sector had made a strategic error in failing to engage with the new funding regime that had facilitated the general renaissance of voluntarism. Classically Christian voluntarism was conducted during the late twentieth century – with some notable exceptions - in the same way that it had in previous centuries, on the basis of self-funding. This had three key implications.

First, from the perspective of church, there had been little appreciation of the extent to which government was funding voluntary bodies in order to address welfare needs. There was thus a distinct lack of understanding of how this was reconstituting the basis of the voluntary sector and facilitating its rapid development. Second, from the perspective of the wider voluntary sector, self-funding had released the Christian Voluntary Sector from the 'partnerships' imperative that increasingly accompanied government grants, giving it the opportunity to become in a real sense 'a voluntary sector apart', disconnected from the wider voluntary sector. Finally, from the perspective of government, self-funding diminished the visibility of the Christian Voluntary Sector because government naturally tends to be primarily concerned – and in practice – ready to listen to the projects that it funds and for whose audit trails it has a responsibility.

By enabling the Christian Voluntary Sector to better engage with funding opportunities the hope was thus to see first increased service provision and second, in the context of the 'partnerships' imperative encountered when pursuing government grants, the development of relationship with the wider voluntary sector. This would greatly enhance local collective capacity in a way that would be mutually beneficial to all concerned. Furthermore, funded by government, the Christian Voluntary Sector would register on the government radar screen.

Representation: Since 2000 Gweini has responded to a number of key consultations and had many meetings with different Assembly Members. In the space available it is only possible to briefly consider some aspects of Gweini's representation work.

In January 2000, the National Assembly launched its consultation regarding the definition of the sustainable development scheme. Gweini responded first by defining its inaugural national conference, 'Wales: A Community of Communities?' (17 March 2000 in Cardiff), around that consultation. Apart from featuring Prof. Sir John Houghton of the UK Sustainable Development Panel, Marjorie Dykins (WCVA), John Osmond (IWA) and Donald Anderson MP, the conference involved a number of Assembly Members. The late Val Feld AM and Janet Ryder AM both addressed the gathering. The event also benefited from a question and answer session with AMs Mick Bates, David Davies and Dai Lloyd. Charles Coombes and Lisa Dobbins of the Sustainable Development Unit were also in attendance.

After the conference Gweini lobbied hard that the Assembly should exploit the incredible opportunity provided by Section 118 of the *Government of Wales Act*, of being practically the only nation in the world with a constitutional responsibility to assess its every move in terms of sustainable development. Gweini maintained that, given the increase in interest in sustainable development, the nation of Wales had been given a tremendous opportunity to *add value* to the development of a global concept which could raise the nation's profile in the wider world. It was good to see this happening at the Sustainable Development Summit in Johannesburg in 2002.

Given the primary concern of the Christian Voluntary Sector with the social environment, Gweini was particularly hoping to see the scheme adopt a more sophisticated definition of the social environment. It also sought to develop clearer mechanisms to empower the Assembly to maximise sustainable outcomes as well as avoid unsustainable outcomes. (See Gweini, *Wales: A Community of Communities*, April 2000.) Gweini's Director and Policy Development Officer had a series of meetings with Assembly Members and civil servants throughout the Summer and Autumn of 2000.

The Spring of 2000, meanwhile, saw the launch of the Assembly's consultation on its ground breaking Communities First policy. Gweini contributed to this process, employing the social environmental approach that informed its work on sustainability. The Assembly drew quite significantly on our submission, quoting directly on a number of occasions in its response to the consultation process. (See National Assembly for Wales, *Regenerating Our Most Disadvantaged Communities: Communities First, Second Consultation Paper – Proposals for Implementation*, December 2000, p. 6, p. 10, p. 23, p. 28.)

Then in 2001 came the *National Economic Development Strategy* consultation and the need to inject a better appreciation of the role of the Christian and wider voluntary sector in the process of economic development. Highlighting the huge economic implications of the voluntary sector in restoring damaged lives doomed, without restorative intervention, to cost the state a vast amount of money, Gweini's submission did much to locate welfare in the context of hard nosed economics. (See www.Gweini.org.uk, policy submissions, *National Economic Development Strategy.*)

Gweini also sought to raise the profile of the Christian Voluntary Sector by working closely with Rev. Aled Edwards, the CYTÛN Assembly Liaison Officer who represents faith communities in the Voluntary Sector Partnership Council. We also participated in some of the related, twice-yearly ministerial meetings. The whole Partnership Council process constitutes an important quasi-constitutional step towards a new and increasingly 'participatory democratic culture' which we have been glad to engage with.

Capacity Building: Capacity building was central to our relationship to the National Assembly since it was in this context that we sought to inform and equip the sector with respect to developments in Cardiff Bay.

During the Autumn of 2000, Gweini was involved with a multi-agency 12 stop national tour which it used to address the opportunities and challenges presented to the Christian Voluntary Sector by the renaissance of the wider voluntary sector. Examining the role of the Christian Voluntary Sector in economic development, these presentations touched on the all important issue of Objective 1, 2 and 3 but they could only whet the appetite. Objective 1 was too big and too important to deal with in the context of seminars about the Christian Voluntary Sector and economic development broadly conceived.

In May 2001, therefore, Gweini hosted three conferences in Rhyl, Swansea and Cardiff called 'The Church and European Funding'. Whilst the Swansea and Rhyl events addressed Objective 1, the Cardiff conference looked at Objective 2 and 3. Including some excellent presentations from the Wales European Funding Office, and (in Rhyl) a visit from Janet Ryder AM, these events drew in people from across the nation and across the denominations who, carrying the knowledge, the pain and aspirations of their own communities, came eager to see how they could help facilitate socio-economic transformation.

Since these events Gweini has also launched its twice-yearly bulletin which addresses funding and policy development matters from a Christian Voluntary Sector perspective. In this it is extremely grateful for the input of Janet Ryder AM, Ann Jones AM and David Melding AM (See Gweini Bulletin Winter 2001/2, Summer 2002 and Spring 2003).

The first four years of the National Assembly have been about engaging with the new democratic interface, impacting policy development and helping the sector understand devolution. In reflecting on the first four years of Wales's first legislature in 600 years the Christian Voluntary Sector - one of the few Welsh institutions that can remember the last Parliaments (!) - has been privileged to play a part in shaping national policy. As we look out across the unknowns of the next four years, filled as they are with latent potentialities, we have great aspirations. Wales needs an Assembly but it also needs a powerful, genuinely diverse, historically rooted, civil society that, with great visions for the future but engaged resolutely with the *now*, can argue with it and sharpen it as 'iron sharpens iron' (Proverbs 27.17). We have endeavored to play our part in this great responsibility that the 'new politics' has placed on civil society and look forward to doing so with even greater vigour during the next four years.

Daniel Boucher is the Gweini Policy Development Officer and also National Assembly Liaison Officer for the interdenominational church umbrella body, the Evangelical Alliance. He has worked for Gweini since its inception and for the Alliance since 1998 first as an Assembly Research Officer and since 1999 as Assembly Liaison Officer. Previously he was a post-graduate student at Swansea University where he worked as a Teaching Assistant for three years in the Politics Department.

A Matter of Faith

By Alan Schwartz

Member of the Inter Faith Council For Wales

Interfaith relationships are hard work. They rely on a personal approach to all nine officially acknowledged faiths of the Interfaith Network UK which is the umbrella organisation that affiliates local Interfaith groups and is a conduit to national government, the press and other agencies.

The problem with getting the interfaith bodies to function is in finding common ground. There are far less concerns when dealing with two faith organisations such as the Council of Christians and Jews, the Maimonides foundation for Muslims and Jews or the Three Faiths Forum for Christians, Muslims and Jews. At least for these three faiths, they have the advantage of being called the Abrahamic faiths and there is a common link. But here is no common theology with Hindus, Sikhs, Buddhists or Jains. So getting them all to work together relies a great deal on goodwill - which is always forthcoming from members of those religions who feel they have common philosophy. This is usually expressed as a commitment to seek to live together in peace and goodwill, to promote respect and tolerance for the integrity of each other's beliefs, cultures and traditions, to recognise their responsibilities to the community, and to urge fellow citizens to put aside intolerance, malice and strife to attain peaceful and fruitful co-operation.

The problems of understanding the beliefs and traditions of various faith groups in Wales is complicated in that, although Wales has had the reputation over the last century as a tolerant society, the whole range of religious communities have never settled widely throughout the country. Thus, Cardiff and to a lesser extent, Swansea and Newport, has had a population consisting of a number of these faiths, though some faiths have dwindled in numbers in these conurbations and are hardly represented. In most of Wales, there is no representation. This can - and has - led to discrimination in some places in Wales such as intolerance of Chinese and Indians working in restaurants, and the reluctance of one town council to consider an application for a mosque.

The case is very strong for building up a tolerant society in Wales where the population has had such a good reputation in the past. There are excellent examples such as that of the Jewish people who came to Cardiff at the end of the 19th Century due to persecution in Europe and Russia and established a thriving and well-liked and respected community. Another well adapted community is that of Muslims who came at about the same time, mainly as a result of the shipping trade, and settled in the docks area of the city. Subsequently, the build-up of other religious groups has assisted the multifaith and multicultural nature of the city. It is now clear that families from different religions and ethnic groups do not necessarily live in the same area, and as they become more affluent, spread throughout the city.

My own experience of interfaith work may be of some note because like all friendly organisations, people of goodwill join because of personal introduction. Unfortunately, the inverse is also true that people of ill-will - those who have their own agenda as in promoting their own religion or in proselytising - also join these organisations.

It has not been unusual to find that, for example, in the Council of Christians and Jews, some have tried to promote Christianity. In interfaith work, there are some who have used the organisation to inculcate religious practices which are anathema to other faiths. It is necessary to guard against such ideas and be aware of those who try to subvert the aims of the organisation as they will undoubtedly alienate others who may want to join, as well as inevitably attract unwelcome press stories.

A friend first introduced me to attending the Cardiff branch of the Council of Christians and Jews (CCJ). The group had been in existence for about 50 years, but apart from surges of interest at various stages, it had become depleted in attendance. There was a resurgence of interest when it was realised that people of note were quite interested to speak at meetings and attend functions. Thus the CCJ was indebted to the late Viscount Tonypandy for his interest and his speaking at a dinner held in his honour about 13 years ago. But more than that, the co-chairpersons at that time were two 'go-ahead' clergy and with the assistance of the Archbishop of Wales, Dr Rowan Williams, the programmes were filled with speakers of national and international note. This undoubtedly attracted large attendances and continues to do so.

For the Cardiff Interfaith organisation, I was phoned by the chairman and asked to attend meetings. I did so, but here there came the sticking point. Because of the variety of beliefs, it was almost impossible to get numbers of people to attend who were not interested in that religious topic. Cardiff Interfaith now has a small committee who guide the programme for the year and though it has had notable success in attracting large crowds for 'important' meetings such as a public signing of religious commitment to the County of Cardiff, the attendance at regular meetings ranges from about 15 to 30 people.

The Interfaith Council for Wales was a nascent body set up over a long period under the inspiration of Dr Mashuq Ally who at that time was head of the Commission for Racial Equality (CRE) in Cardiff. Essentially his ideas were larger than the small committee could encapsulate. There would be an office in the centre of Cardiff which could be manned and he planned several sub-committees which were apportioned to various members to take care of. Slow progress was made setting this up but the whole project was overtaken by 11 September 2001. As a reaction to the disastrous events in New York, First Minister Rhodri Morgan decided to call a meeting of political leaders in Wales together with representatives from all the faith communities - at least all those who could be contacted. This resulted in the setting up of the Welsh Inter Faith Council with meetings planned for twice a year. In attendance would be faith representatives (one or two from each non-Christian faith and more from the Christians) together with all party political leaders in Wales and a sprinkling of civil servants.

The First Minister admitted that setting up the council was a reaction to a rise in inter community tension as manifested in attacks on Muslims or those thought to be Muslims. He noted the wish of those attending for a better interface with the police. Similarly, he had been to a meeting with the Society of Editors of newspapers and it was accepted that issues around race and religion required sensitive handling. Although it was stressed that Welsh rural areas were under-represented, they would be kept informed. The work of the Council was connected to that of the Voluntary Sector Partnership Council.

The Inter Faith Council of Wales thus became a 'sub-committee' of the Welsh Assembly and needed to have a link with the umbrella body for the UK - The Interfaith Network UK. Unlike the equivalents in Ireland and Scotland which were independent, The Welsh Interfaith Council, being a 'sub-committee' of the Assembly has a different relationship from the others. However, the up-side is that it is effectively run by the civil service and exists on a formal basis. Meetings are regularly held which are well minuted and decisions can immediately be referred to Interfaith Network UK. For reasons unconnected with the Welsh Interfaith Council, I am a member of the executive of the Interfaith Network UK. I am regarded as the Welsh representative on the executive body of the Interfaith Network UK.

One item which has been dealt with on the Welsh Interfaith Council is the issue of faith schools. This is predominantly a Muslim project at the moment as it is the only non Christian faith with sufficient children to consider setting up a school(s). There is already a Muslim Junior school which has 80 pupils though 250 have applied. Clearly there is a need in the area but it is not the policy of the Assembly to set up faith schools but to argue the case for their existence.

The topic of Religious Holidays was introduced and this is an item that affects many non-Christian faiths. Whereas, parents may observe religious holidays by withdrawing their children from school by arrangement with the Headteacher, the proposition was that 2.5 days should be allowed for religious holidays in addition to the statutory ones.

Other topics for consideration were matters such as religious discrimination and religious festivals in school life.

The Interfaith Network UK holds 3 meetings year and is very active with an office and staff in central London and is under the leadership of Brian Pearce OBE. The Co-chairpersons are Rt. Rev Tom Butler, Bishop of Southwark, and Mrs Rosalind Preston OBE Their work covers almost all aspects of faith requirements and interfaith relationships.

A recent symposium covered the following topics and presentations: - social cohesion from a national point of view; local social cohesion; reflections and responses of the beliefs and concerns of others; a report on the Welsh Interfaith Council; workshops on working towards greater social cohesion.

It is probably true that any organisation can justify its existence by numerous initiatives, meetings or social interaction. The Interfaith bodies at local level, all-Wales, and at national level lead one to realise that there are great changes occurring throughout faith communities which are being recognised at the local political level, by the Welsh Assembly, by government as well as by Royalty. The immediate prospects for a healthier religious life for Wales and the UK have been instituted over the last few years and auger well for the future of active support for individual faiths and for much improved interfaith relationships.

Alan Schwartz serves the Jewish community on the Interfaith Council for Wales.

The Refugee Doctors' Group

By Leona Evans

Displaced People in Action Project Worker

When a person becomes an asylum seeker, it's as though all their qualities, characteristics and achievements are stripped off, as if they were to forget their past and brace their future as new-borns. Their support workers and other officials they deal with only see them as dependants. I am told that for asylum seekers who are educated and have years of experience in their fields of expertise, this time of being a non-entity is unbearable. They spend their time waiting for the asylum claim to be decided, going to court, worrying about the future, pining for their family, friends, possessions and lives they had to leave behind. Some become totally demoralised and once they receive their decision, have no desire to regain their past employment status. Fortunately the majority do not loose hope.

In my work with Displaced People in Action (DPIA) I meet people like this every day. Lawyers, accountants, teachers, lecturers, office workers, computer engineers, are just some of the highly trained professionals DPIA encounters. One of the professions that seemed to surface more and more frequently among our clients was medical doctor. At first I found five doctors from different medical and geographical backgrounds. They came to DPIA separately asking for help to relieve the boredom and to take their mind off their situation.

To be accepted by the General Medical Council (GMC) and to be able to practice in Britain, a person coming from overseas must pass three examinations.

ILETS, the International English Language Testing System became a pre-requisite for admission to the PLAB test. Doctors must achieve an overall 7.0 with a minimum of 6.0 in all the categories. The test is extremely difficult; many native English speakers would have trouble with it. The course to prepare for this test cost over £1,000 and each test costs £78. If one fails the test it takes three months before one can take another test. Very few people pass the first time.

The PLAB examinations assess the professional and linguistic suitability of an overseas doctor to practice in this country. The standard required to pass the test is defined in the following terms: 'A candidate's command of the English language and professional knowledge and skill must be shown to be sufficient for him or her to undertake safely employment at first year Senior House Officer level in a British hospital.' Before granting limited registration to an overseas-qualified doctor, the GMC must have the assurance that the doctor has the professional knowledge and skill and the knowledge of English, necessary for medical practice in the United Kingdom.

PLAB 1, providing you are a refugee, you will be exempt from paying the PLAB 1 Test fee for the first two attempts. The preparation course however costs £630 and is only offered outside of Wales so for our Welsh refugee doctors the expense mounts up with travel and accommodation. The PLAB 2 preparation course is offered in Cardiff and costs £195 but the PLAB 2 examination cost £430 and a trip to London or Manchester. Finally the registration costs £390. You may think: "That's OK, they are doctors they can afford it!" But don't forget that these doctors are not receiving salaries, are either dependant on state benefit because they cannot find a job as no one will employ them, or work for very low wage. I tried every avenue I could think of but received no offers of assistance.

Soon the group expanded to 13 doctors begging me to help them get back to work in their professions. I could not believe that in Wales, there was not a system in place to access this greatly needed resource. In England there are organisations set up to provide financial assistance. This doesn't extend to Wales. As a result 4 doctors left to live in London. One doctor, found a job as a factory worker as he felt that he had to provide for his family. He said that on his salary it would take so long to save up the money for the courses and the exams that he would have forgotten everything.

The Vice Chair of DPIA, Aled Edwards, was as frustrated about the issue as I was and brought it to the attention of the National Assembly for Wales and Dr. B K Bhowmick, Associate Dean for the Overseas Doctors in Wales. Dr Bhowmick, a former refugee, empathised with the group and soon the doors were opening. The group expanded through word of mouth resulting in 22 refugee doctors registering with us. We set up several meetings, looking at the individual needs of our clients and researched the resources available.

In September 2002 we received £73,600 from the National Assembly for Wales for the refugee doctors' re-qualification programme.

The programme began immediately. We set up a medical library at the DPIA Drop In Centre, which includes English language textbooks as well as examples of past exams for doctors, and run a study group. The ESOL department at Bridgend College were already offering ILETS preparation courses and wanted to concentrate on doctors. The staff and management of the college are very dedicated and go beyond their duties to help the students succeed. The refugee doctors who are preparing for the ILETS exam receive a travel card to and from the college to attend the classes. The tutor assesses the ability of each individual before they can register for the exam.

DPIA have made connections with the PLAB 1 and 2 course centres, making administrative arrangements for payments. The doctors are to register for the exams and their fee is reimbursed.

To date we have two doctors who are now working in the NHS in Wales. One passed the last exam in December, 2002 and is looking for an attachment. Seventeen are still studying for the ILETS exam. Five are due to take the ILETS exam in February 2003. One doctor is registered for PLAB 1 course in April and for the test in May and two doctors are ready to register for the PLAB 2 course and exam.

Medical doctors are very frequent among asylum seekers coming to Britain. The Home Office dispersal scheme with Cardiff County Council is coming up to its second year in

April 2003. There are a constant number of about 1000 asylum seekers on this scheme. There are other providers of accommodation who have private Home Office dispersal schemes. Swansea Council has recently begun their dispersal scheme. There are also private providers in the area. Other places with private dispersal schemes are Newport and Wrexham. So the number of potential refugees who will be highly qualified increases.

To date, in Cardiff alone, about 30 of the asylum seeker populations have been identified as doctors. Some have moved away from Wales after they received their refugee status. We anticipate that over the next year our Refugee Doctors Group will at least triple in membership and will need to cater to refugee doctors all over Wales.

Refugee doctors are an untapped source of employees for the NHS. They are hungry for work. Most, being single, are willing to relocate even to rural areas. To educate a High School Graduate to become a medical doctor costs thousands and thousands of pounds with a high 'drop out' rate. To re-educate a refugee doctor costs approximately £3,600. The 'drop out' rate is zero.

On behalf of the Refugee Doctors Group I would like to thank all the people who have made the re-training for the doctors possible and to the National Assembly for Wales for the funding which allows doctors to re-qualify, re-employ and re-build lives.

We hope that in the future this service will be extended to other occupations.

Leona Evans has been seconded by DPIA to work with the National Assembly on the refugee doctor project.

Setting Prisoners Free

By Helen Mary Jones

Plaid Cymru Assembly Member for Llanelli

The Assembly's Equal Opportunities Committee has been clear from the start that we will not confine our deliberations either to devolved matters, or to equality matters covered by current legislation. We have taken the view that the Assembly's 'absolute duty' to promote equality of opportunity for all as enshrined in the *Government of Wales Act* gives us the right and the responsibility to seek out injustice and inequality wherever in manifests itself in Wales and expose it, with a view to ensuring that whoever is responsible for righting the wrongs identified gets on with doing so!.

It was not surprising, then, that when the plight of asylum seekers incarcerated in Cardiff Prison came to the notice of the public in April 2001 the Committee decided to instigate an investigation into the position on asylum seekers in Wales, despite immigration and asylum being non devolved matters. What followed was a credit to our new democracy, and I am personally proud of having played some small part in a process that I believe ultimately had influence beyond our borders.

I don't propose to try to give here a full chronology of events. Rather I will set out to give a personal perspective on how the issue was dealt with, and some comments on what I believe it tells us about the potential of the Assembly.

Briefly, what happened was this. The Minster, Edwina Hart, responded to questions from members about the incarceration of asylum seekers. The Minster made a Statement to the full Assembly on the factual position that on that day, 3rd of May 2001: there were 17 asylum seekers in Cardiff Prison, 14 waiting to hear the outcome of there appeals and three waiting to hear about there original claims. She made it plain that this was not a position that she was content with, far from it. She made it clear she was not in the business of defending the indefensible!

The Committee began an investigation, and the Minster began what I think she would happy to describe as a robust dialogue with ministers at Westminster. It would be true to say that many of the original, and subsequent questions asked came as no surprise to the Minster. From the start that this was a matter on which the whole Assembly, across party lines, were agreed. The role of the Conservative Group, particularly William Graham and David Melding, was commendable and striking, and could not have been more different that the approach being taken by there fellow Tories at Westminster. Indeed, this was fast becoming a matter of the Assembly v. Westminster.

The Minster secured the attendance of a senior Home Office official at a meeting of the Equal opportunities Committee on the 11th of July. Of course, this was quite a coup in itself. There is no formal sense in which the Home Office is accountable to the Assembly. I suspect that Edwina Hart used a combination of the moral authority conferred by full Assembly backing, force of personality, and sheer bloody mindedness to persuade the

Home Office Ministers to let us quiz the deputy director of the Detention Services Directorate of the UK Immigration Service. At any rate, there he was.

During the same meeting, and before, we had heard gut wrenching testimony from inside the prison. Asylum seekers taken straight from the airport to Cardiff Prison convinced they were on their way to execution, since that was what the were facing at home. A thousand petty humiliations. The stigma of being treated like a criminal in the very land in which you had sought protection and freedom. And we had heard of the day to day shame of asylum seeking families shopping with vouchers, stigmatized. We also heard that day from lawyers and campaigners, there on an equal footing with Mr. David Wilson of the Home Office.

Committee members were in no mood to take any nonsense from the Home Office. The Minster had already secured a commitment from Westminster that there would be no more asylum seekers in Cardiff Prison by October. When Mr Wilson made a chance remark that suggested that December was the deadline the Committee made our views very plain. As we discussed the Westminster government's plans for 'dispersal' and the voucher system, I felt almost sorry for him. To see him relax as David Melding was called as Conservative spokesperson to ask a question, and to see his obvious confusion and near panic when the Tory he expected to be 'on his side' gently and forensically demolished his arguments and exposed the weaknesses at the heart of the system, would have been pitiful had not the issues at stake been so important.

That day the Committee, supported by the Minster, and with the weight of the whole Assembly behind us, left poor Mr Wilson, and Tony Blair's Government, in no doubt where Wales stood on issue of immigration and asylum. The final comments made by Janet Ryder AM are worth quoting, since they summed up the views of us all:

> To be completely honest, Chair, I am shocked by what we have heard this morning. I'm shocked that it seems to be government policy to accommodate people in prison without any assessment of those people first being made. I cannot accept that this is a positive way for a civilised society to deal with people who have come to this country to seek help and safety. It is not acceptable.

By the Autumn there were no more asylum seekers in Cardiff Prison. Not long afterwards the Westminster government announced major u turns in asylum policy - no more vouchers, no more prison, and a complete change in dispersal policy. Not that the policy is right now. Far from it. But important steps in the right direction. I believe that the National Assembly, speaking for Wales, played an important part in forcing those u turns, and I'm proud and glad we did.

Looking back, it is hard to believe how angry many of us were to hear in April 2001 of innocent asylum seekers being taken handcuffed from Cardiff Prison to hospital for treatment. The image of people who had come to our nation, often fleeing deadly peril, to seek safety being imprisoned then exposed to public view in chains was, and remains, almost unbearable, conjuring up as it does memories of the disgraceful legacy of slavery But it is hard to believe how angry we were because we - the politicians, the press and the community more widely - should have known what was going on. The fact is we did not.

I was aware that asylum seekers were occasionally held in prison, but I had believed this was only while awaiting deportation following a full appeals process, and only then when there was a substantial and proven risk of absconding. I believe that perspective was widely shared among my fellow Assembly Members. We were shocked to discover what was really going on.

It is interesting to note that this shock and anger was shared across Civil society in Wales. The *South Wales Echo*, for example, reported the imprisonment issue with an intelligence and compassion in stark contrast to the borderline racist hysteria about asylum issues in some elements of the English regional press.

I have already mentioned the stance of the Conservatives in Wales. The Labour Group, including the Cabinet were prepared to dissociate themselves form Blair and Blunkett. We in Plaid Cymru were able to stand with other parties, strong in our deeply held internationalist traditions. The Minster was ready to work co-operatively with other parties, and with campaigning groups, regardless of party political interest, concerned with getting the right result, and I believe unafraid of treading on toes to get it.

This was an example of the National Assembly at its best. This was the Assembly speaking for the people of Wales, over an issue over which we have no power, and exerting enormous influence. This was the Assembly standing up for those least able to stand up for themselves, in the finest tradition of Welsh radical politics. And this was the Assembly challenging central government on a matter of principal and winning.

I became a nationalist because I believe that Welsh political culture is different. I supported the Assembly because even though it falls far short of the proper Parliament to which Wales is entitled I believed it could do good - if only in giving a voice to that culture. I campaigned for the equality clauses in the *Government of Wales Act* because I believed they would give the Assembly a sound legal base for tackling injustice. And I believed that it would be possible in the Assembly to find common cause and to act for change across Party lines, when the issue was important enough.

As an opposition member and a Shadow Cabinet Minster of course there have been times when I have felt hugely frustrated by the unwillingness of the National Assembly Government to challenge Westminster, to take risks to speak out on behalf of the people of Wales. But there have been other times when I have been hugely encouraged, and even proud, of how we have used our young democracy. The way we handled the asylum issue was certainly one of these.

In how we responded to asylum, and in other ways, the Assembly has, in its first three and a half years proved its worth. But this is just a beginning. If we have done good with the little power we have, think how much more good we could do with more. These three years have proved that the Assembly can be the foundation of a true democracy for Wales. Surely it is now time to build on that foundation.

Helen Mary Jones is a former Senior Development Manager with the Equal Opportunities Commission in Wales. Born in 1960 she is the Plaid Cymru Shadow Education and Lifelong Learning Minister and Spokesperson on Equal Opportunities. She has worked in worked with public and voluntary sectors and a former member of the National Assembly Advisory Group. Her voluntary interests have included work for Welsh Women's Aid.

No More Porridge?

Community Chaplaincy at Swansea Prison

By David Emery

Each journey begins with the first step, the journey of Community Chaplaincy in HMP Swansea started even before the 'phrase' Community Chaplaincy was even heard of. Every Prison in England and Wales needs to conform to the *1952 Prisons Act*, which states that a Governor, Doctor and Chaplain have to be in post in every prison to provide holistic care for each inmate. HMP Swansea conformed to that requirement by the provision of Chaplaincy cover via a team of local Church leaders visiting on a rota basis. With the appointment of Rev. Lionel Hopkins in 1996 as Chaplain, this team ministry flourished to the extent that following the Chief Inspectors of Prisons, Sir David Ramsbottom's *1999 Inspection Report,* Rev. Hopkins was made the first full time Chaplain of HMP Swansea in response to Sir David's recommendations.

In parallel to this appointment, Vicky O'Dea, Wales' first female Governor in Charge took over the Governorship at HMP Swansea. Within the next 12 months the idea of Community Chaplaincy flourished within the seven strong Chaplaincy Team encouraged and supported by Governor O'Dea. The lament of all the Chaplains centred on the return of inmates who, having served their time would be released, soon re-offend and return to prison. Was Community Chaplaincy an answer to this predicament?

The Correctional Services of Canada in the 1980's recognised a similar pattern of re-offending, one answer was the concept of Community Chaplaincy. Their idea was to continue the work that the Prison Chaplain would have done with an inmate on the 'inside' to the 'outside', thus helping to reduce re-offending and create a safer community for everyone. Originating from this idea the Correctional Services of Canada now have a nationwide network of Community Chaplains servicing both Federal and Provincial Prisons.

Prison Chaplaincy Headquarters introducing Community Chaplaincy to the UK audience arranged a national conference. Both Rev. Lionel Hopkins and I attended the conference; we left knowing that the concept of 'Community Chaplaincy' could work at HMP Swansea – Why? We recognised that as one poet so observantly quoted, 'Swansea is a collection of villages held together by Gossip'. There is still 'community' in the areas where the majority of the inmates at HMP Swansea return to and within those neighbourhoods there are faith communities who with some encouragement could provide the necessary support the released prisoner may need on release.

The next 12 months saw the development of the idea into a formal proposal. This proposal was the end product of countless advice, discussions and research. It was vital that all facets of the idea were subject to consultation – ranging from inmates, HMP staff, Faith communities, statutory agencies to Politicians. Without exception the feedback received during this consultative period indicated a willingness to support this innovative concept. Major breakthroughs in respect to The Salvation Army's willingness to allow me to pilot the idea through, provision of accommodation for my family by the Methodist Church. We were pleasantly surprised at the way we had access and then the attention of David A'Hearne and senior personnel in the Crime Reduction unit at the Welsh Assembly Government. We were very grateful for the sound and sensible advice given.

In tandem to all the paperwork, discussions and formulation of the proposal, a personal application to the Millennium Award Scheme for me to find out first hand what Community Chaplaincy in Canada was like, was accepted. Consultation with the Correctional Services of Canada enabled a month long trip to Canada to take place in June 2001. This was an opportunity to see first hand the impact of the initiative we were embarking upon in the land of its birth. Whistle-stop visits to Quebec, Toronto, Vancouver, Victoria, Edmonton, Fredericton and Amherst, equipped me with a working understanding of Community Chaplaincy in Canada from the Atlantic to Pacific coasts.

Meanwhile back in the UK we were still searching for funding for this new initiative. As a result of the Welsh Assembly Government interest, doors were opened into the Local Authorities Crime Reduction / Community Safety Unit, here we found our greatest allies. Les Jones, the Swansea Community Safety Co-ordinator saw the value of such a scheme and assisted in shaping our proposals into a viable application for funding targeting the new 'Communities Against Drugs' initiative. All the necessary criteria for such funding were met; we waited just a few months before we heard in November 2001 that funding for the project would be made available until March 2004.

The idea now needed implementing; thankfully the support and co-operation of the Governor, Senior Management Team and Staff at HMP Swansea allowed the idea to formulate into what is now the UK standard for Community Chaplaincy. Volunteers from the Faith Communities were identified, scrutinised and trained into a body of willing helpers centring their efforts on released prisoners and their needs in the first three months of freedom. A major ingredient to the success of the project has always been recognising that partnership is essential. No one person, agency or body can provide everything, however, together the various bodies can present a package that may assist the released prisoner with the tools to start afresh and break the cycle of crime.

Windows of opportunity do present themselves, albeit infrequently. A chance conversation with the Development Manager of the Swansea YMCA, Tanya Hewson indicated that within the YMCA building was a residential unit currently in 'moth balls'. Actively working with prisoners due to be released I was aware of many inmates who benefited from their time in Prison by addressing their problems of addiction. For many, their addiction had created a lifestyle likened to total chaos. The structure of prison life had assisted in their detoxification and for some an opportunity to make a life changing decision with respect to their addiction by entering the Rehab Unit recently opened in HMP Swansea.

It is essential that support be provided for these changed individuals on release. Their new way of life is in total contrast to their lifestyle pre prison, unless support is available, their chances of remaining clean and crime-free are slim. What was needed was a location for these reformed people to be supported and eased back into community, whilst adopting their chosen new lifestyle. Was the 'mothballed' Residential Unit an answer to this dilemma? Within a few days I visited the YMCA and recognised the potential of the idea now germinating in my mind. A few weeks later an initial group of interested people gathered at the YMCA, potential partners in the scheme we now call Gorwelion [Horizon]. Approval and enthusiasm from these 'Partners' fuelled the idea; it was not such a 'hair-brained scheme' after all. It was time to formalise and mobilise the right people into producing a feasible plan.

The initial working party consisted of delegates from bodies who could contribute to the core idea of Gorwelion. Governor Brian Taylor (HMP Swansea), Jill Lewis (Probation and Prison Throughcare), Mike Hardy (HMP Prison Service Area Drugs Manager for Wales), Les Jones (Community Safety Co-ordinator - City and County of Swansea), Rev. Lionel Hopkins (Chaplaincy HMP Swansea), John Holtam (Salvation Army Substance Misuse Advisor), Major Alison Thompson (Salvation Army Director for Social Work-South Wales), Russell Davies (Research and Development Consultant- Salvation Army UK), Sarah Vye (Housing Dept.- City and County of Swansea), Tanya Hewson (YMCA Swansea-Development Officer). These good people with myself acting as chair initiated the necessary progress in making the idea become a reality.

Within the next six months many hours of background research was accomplished, formulating the 'proposal'. The modularity of the adopted programme, the target group who would be suitable to the modularity, assessment of suitable candidates, who would not be suitable due to certain previous criminal activity and most importantly what contingencies would be in place for residents to move on from Gorwelion. Encompassed in the programme modularity was all the practical issues relating to the working/residing environment of Gorwelion. New legislation affected room sizes, en-suite facilities were needed, disability access etc. etc. such factors needed consideration. A professional assessment of the location including working architectural drawings and costing related to those drawings were needed. The project team were extremely grateful to Huw Griffiths Architects who undertook the initial feasibility study relating to the necessary building work.

It was important to bring the existing structure up to current standards in tandem with the intricacies that the programme modularity demanded. An innovative holistic plan was created with a light, airy feel to the living and working environment of Gorwelion. Provision of a lift to access the fourth floor plus furnishings and fittings that would enhance the central aims of the project was demonstrated. Bob Tovey, Quantity Surveyor undertook the unenviable task of costing out the scheme, resulting in a figure balancing around the £400,000 mark. If it was not for the work undertaken by all the above mentioned people free of charge the proposal which was now ready for submission to the Welsh Assembly Government would not have been reached.

During the copious meetings held in the lead up to this point, Mike Hardy had kept the Crime Reduction Unit at the Welsh Assembly Government informed of developments. It was now time to 'test the water' and discover the Assembly's view on the progress made concerning Gorwelion. Every twist and turn of the project to this point of time had rested on the hope that when everything that could be done locally to provide an informed scenario of what was proposed, a 'benefactor' would see its value and earth the dream with an injection of capital. The accessibility, advice and sheer interest of the

Assembly once again heartened and inspired us.

The rhetoric evolved into action when Finance Minister Edwina Hart announced a visit to HMP Swansea. She wanted to see for herself the opportunities available to those who had an addiction problem whilst incarcerated. The Minister arrived, after a short briefing period concerning the current opportunities in the prison as well as the aims and objectives that Gorwelion may offer, her delegation toured the prison. On that tour the Minister and her party saw first hand what was being achieved inside the walls and listened to the inmates tell of their chaotic life styles prior to imprisonment. Rapt attention was paid when inmates told how the Rehab programme was sorting out their addictions and lifestyle but also how they had fears for the future when released and their need for 24/7 support. In as much that the proposal paperwork was important in presenting the aims of Gorwelion, the words of desperate inmates carried far more authority than could be recorded on paper. The Minister left with a clear understanding of the problem and a promise to look into our proposals.

True to her word Finance Minister Edwina Hart considered our proposals and a month later announced that she would support this innovative project that we all had been working towards for the last 12 months. £400,000 would be made available for capital costs towards helping ex-offenders with drink and drug issues in the provision of a supported accommodation unit in Swansea. Gorwelion had now received the financial backing we were looking for. Within a few weeks we met with the necessary civil servants at the Welsh Assembly Government to formulate a way forward to tie up all the necessary conditions and safeguards that such a substantial grant entails. As I write these details are being finalised, within a few weeks as the new financial year dawns we anticipate being able to instruct the Architects to make their more detailed plans, obtain structural surveys, put the building work out to tender thus transforming a 'mothballed' residential unit into Wales' first supported accommodation for ex-offenders with addiction problems.

Whether it's Community Chaplaincy or Gorwelion ... the work continues, often it is of the 'bread and butter' variety, un-spectacular, seemingly mundane yet for the individual a lifeline in breaking free from the cycle of crime and its related associations. Is Community Chaplaincy the panacea for recidivism in our communities? No, however the data we have produced thus far show positive trends, positive for the inmate, his family as well as the neighbours in the community he returns to. Speculation indicates that within the span of the pilot project 200+ individuals will have asked for assistance in the first three months of their release, that assistance can vary in intensity, yet it is the assistance that just maybe the difference between 'staying out' or returning to prison at a cost of £65,000 a year courtesy of the Tax Payer.

The Social Exclusion Unit's Report *Reducing Rre-offending by Ex-prisoners* (July 2002) states: - 'An ex-prisoner's path back to prison is extremely costly for the criminal justice system. A re-offending ex-prisoner is likely to be responsible for crime costing the criminal justice system an average of £65,000. Prolific offenders will cost even more. When re-offending leads to a further prison sentence, the costs soar. The average cost of a prison sentence imposed at a crown court is roughly £30,500, made up of court and other legal costs. The costs of actually keeping prisoners within prison vary significantly, but average £37,500 per year. And yet these costs are only a fraction of the overall cost of re-offending.'

Our journey thus far has comprised of many types of steps, some small others like giant leaps, some hesitant shuffles others bold and deliberate; yet each step makes up the ground we have covered thus far. The journey continues, each new step may seem insignificant yet it is a step firmly planted in the desire that for those who currently find themselves behind bars, there is hope – hope for a new start, a new future - one which may be assisted by the work of the Swansea Community Chaplaincy Project which is supported directly or indirectly by the Welsh Assembly Government but defiantly assisted by the One who specialises in change and is the motivation for the journey.

David Emery was born in the Rhondda Valley and educated at Porth County Grammar School and SGIHE. For 5 years he worked for the NHS as a Clinical Chemist. In 1982, left the NHS and entered the *International Training College*, London to be trained as a Salvation Army Officer. Following commissioning (ordination) he ministered in north Wales for 10 years specifically concentrating on church planting. A move to Aberystwyth followed where ministry centred on the churches response to unemployment and the environment. In 1997 he was given specific responsibility for the work of The Salvation Army in the City Centre of Swansea. That ensued until the current post of Community Chaplain developed in June 2001. He is currently studying 'Addictive Behaviour' with the University of Kent attempting to become equipped in the field of crime and alcohol/drug misuse. He is married to Michele, has four noisy children (18, 16, 14, 10) and enjoys watching the Whites (Swansea RFC) and detests any form of gardening!

Communities First

By Kathryn Price

Park United Reformed Church, Llanelli

At a time when there appeared to be a different forum for every possible human activity, Communities First came like a breath of fresh air. A glance through any community activist's diary would illustrate the problem: a different meeting for each interest – the arts, youth and children and family concerns, health and well-being. Then there is the area community forum and its task groups. Alongside this plethora of 'talking shops' came the suspicion that unless one was part of these 'chattering classes', funding would be difficult to come by. So time is taken up going from venue to venue, meeting more or less the same people, if in different combinations, each looking for the best deal for their own organisation. You have to have your project in the 'apple' to be considered for European money; you have to be in another group even to hear about some funding opportunities. How can we find the time to actually do some real work?

Yet despite all this apparent togetherness, the goal of uniqueness is the ultimate aim. We need to comply with the 'additionality' requirements of funders; however along with this uniqueness can come an overdeveloped sense of one's importance in the great scheme of things.

Then along came Communities First. A programme where the needs of the community would be more important than those of the groups working there. A programme that would cover all aspects of life in that place – housing, health, play, arts, sports, transport, environment. A programme, moreover, that included 'faith communities' in its list of those to be involved. Joined-up thinking for community activism!

As a church with a community project, Communities First seemed like the answer to prayer. We have always aimed for an holistic approach to the community in which we are set, aiming to feed minds and spirits as well as bodies. Partnership too has always been our chosen way of working; time and money are too short for reinvention, if someone is already doing a good job at making wheels.

It came as a pleasant surprise for faith groups to have a mention in the discussion paper. Churches across the country are involved in a range of community activities, using their premises for luncheon clubs, after-school clubs, playgroups, drop-in centres, family contact centres; the list goes on. Similarly it is church members who make up a large proportion of volunteers working with other groups and charities. Despite this, it is unlikely for churches to be invited to be part of the forums mentioned above. We have become involved through our community project, which has its own name and identity, but others are ignored.

It has to be admitted that churches have colluded to create this invisibility by not considering themselves to be part of the voluntary sector. This is to be regretted as not only do churches lose out on a whole range of information, not to mention funding, which could help them in their mission work, but also the community misses the opportunity to involve committed folk and useful premises in their development.

There is also the suspicion with which some secular bodies view churches, assuming that 'bums on pews' is the only factor in their community work. It is true that some are more evangelical in their intention than others, but to tar all with the same brush is a prejudice which needs challenging.

There is a further, more internal, problem that comes into play, when a church seeks to become involved in its community. Where that community is a very small town, or village, it is not so obvious – most of the members live in the community in question. Where the church is in a larger town, the only one of its denomination, it becomes clearer – most churches are gathered congregations. Most of them may live in completely different parts of town and when the focus is on the immediately surrounding area, then it is often difficult to engage the membership in the community work. Even those churches with recognised parishes find that their parish is not co-terminus with the wards in question and a certain amount of boundary crossing is inevitable.

There have been a range of issues to be addressed as Communities First has begun to establish itself. The first is that, despite all the trumpeting, it is not the be-all and end-all of community work. There are other bodies with roles to play – local authorities, community forums (still), other statutory bodies. It is taking a while for all involved to be clear which body is responsible for what – one of the results of the "usual suspects" being at each different event!

Then there is a suspicion that what we are doing is setting up yet another organisation, with staff and offices, but no real strategy as yet. Will this organisation create new activities or support and co-ordinate those groups already in existence? Another anomaly exists in the Communities First Trust fund to which groups can apply, by-passing the local partnership board, thus undermining a real attempt at a co-ordinated approach.

There is already a feeling that groups are relocating - moving into Communities First wards, because funding will be easier to secure and a certain amount of envy, though not yet hostility, from those outside the selected wards. In a town like Llanelli, where ward boundaries are not obvious, this may cause serious problems in the future, especially for groups with a wider brief than just the one ward. There is after all a certain irony in the poorest wards becoming the most sought-after locations!

Hopes are high, though. The greatest hope is that by working together, boundaries will become blurred and divisions broken down between the different sectors – statutory and voluntary, faith group and secular organisation, education and entertainment. Regeneration is the name of the game and these wards have a long way to go before they become somewhere people actively want to live and work. We need to take the long view. If we avoid the trap of the quick-fix approach, then these communities will become models of co-ordinated community support that should be replicated in other wards sooner, rather than later and a holistic approach to human development – meeting spiritual needs as well as physical and educational – will become the norm.

Kathryn Price was ordained in 1997 in Llanelli, where the possibility of some kind of community project had been discussed with Social Services. Her background is mixed – ante-natal teacher with the National Childbirth Trust, theatre administration, youth and community theatre wardrobe, animation festival director, day care organiser for Age Concern – so she has a range of experiences to draw on, apart from a deep conviction that every church has a mission to its local community. Five years on, they have a Church-Related Community Worker – Judy Harris, a community café, stained glass workshop, arts classes, music nights, martial arts groups, Tools for Self-reliance, a community garden; they work in partnership with Artscare, Lynx workshops, Llanelli Youth Theatre, a new healthy living project, BTCV, youth justice and others. Funding is still a problem and the building is still in need of renovation, but they are convinced, and confirmed in that conviction by others, that they are on the right track, being church in community, and live and work in hope.

The Community That Refused to Die

By Keith T. O'Brien
Chair of Traws-Newid

Trawsfynydd, Gwynedd, where I live is a small upland village. The parish covers 12,830 hectares and has a population of about 1,000 mostly Welsh speaking people. I am a local government officer, a Community Councillor and the Chair of Traws-Newid, a community company run by local people. Traws-Newid was set up in the wake of the closure of Trawsfynydd's Nuclear Power Station, with a view to improving the economic, social and environmental aspects of the community.

The closure of the power station was indisputably a major blow to the area. Not only in respect of losing well paid and highly skilled jobs, but also something that is sometimes ignored, the loss of the community's confidence, often only indicated by tumbling or low house prices, closed shops and increased vandalism - the veneer of a community stripped of its self-esteem and civic pride.

This was the scenario facing the community back in the mid-nineties. But, what made it worse was the fact that in the past there had always been portents of good fortune that showed promise for the future. Both World Wars ensured a huge influx of soldiers to the Battle Training Camp at the nearby hamlet of Bronaber, from 1904 to 1956, which created direct civilian employment as well as indirect through cafes, laundries, etc.

In the meantime, in 1926, the North Wales Power Company, to act as a reservoir for the Maentwrog hydroelectric power station, created Wales' third largest lake near the village. Again, providing much-needed jobs through its construction.

With the closure of the military camp in 1956, came further employment opportunities with the building of two canals, to supply additional waters to the lake. This was a precursor to the construction of the country's only in-land nuclear power station, which was commissioned in 1965 and provided employment for 600 people in its heyday. When the announcement came in the early nineties that the plant was to be decommissioned, the ingredient that had always been there in the past was now missing i.e. new job opportunities for the economic well-being of the community.

What were we to do? When the nation needed a hero during the First World War, didn't they turn to communities such as Trawsfynydd, who gave one of her sons - Hedd Wyn. He won the chair of the National Eisteddfod in 1917, but was killed on the battlefield before he could claim it. To whom was Traws, now arguably in her greatest hour of need going to turn? The answer was simple – by taking the future into our own hands. After all, the parish could trace its history back over 1,400 years, and it certainly wasn't ready to throw the towel in just yet!

The Community Council cast the die in 1995 when it set up an Improvements Sub-committee, whose main purpose then was to undertake a Community Appraisal. This was a daunting task, however; the Sub-committee had two distinct advantages, which would help secure the success of its mission. Firstly the majority of the members were new, young and enthusiastic. Secondly with nearly fifty years experience at County, District and Community Council level, the invaluable guidance and expertise of Councillor Isgoed Williams.

February 1996 saw the Committee Members, together with volunteers, door-knocking every home in the parish with a questionnaire for each family member from the age of twelve upwards. In a fortnight's time they would return to collect them and assist with any difficult parts. This ensured an 84% return rate, providing an unprecedented amount of information about the community's hopes, aspirations, concerns and worries across a broad spectrum of subjects, such as, tourism, employment, services, etc. "In the land of the blind, the one-eyed man is King", or so the saying goes. To this end it was good to receive the assistance of the former Meirionnydd District Council, Antur Dwyryd-Llyn, Cymad and Jigso, in deciphering the information so that we had a coherent report to present to the community.

The report was ready by November and was discussed at a series of public meetings, so that priorities and mandates could be received from the community – full consultation being the watchword. The strength of this exercise was its bottom-up approach with the parish airing its own opinions on its own future – not the thoughts of outside consultants 'parachuted' in to tell us what was best for our community. Two clear priorities came out of these meetings. Firstly, to do something about the redundant Co-op store in the centre of the village, which was now a target for vandals. Secondly, to open up talks with BNFL Magnox with regard to developing the lake, for tourism and leisure purposes.

Both projects received the immediate support of the various funding bodies, particularly the Welsh Development Agency (WDA), Gwynedd Council and indeed BNFL Magnox. However, one problem reared its head, Community Councils, generally, cannot make grant applications, albeit that a sub-committee could, and these two projects were going to need an awful lot of grant assistance if they were to be realised! The way forward was to create a community company limited by warranty.

Therefore, 1998 not only saw the advent of the Assembly, but also Traws-Newid Ltd.! Traws-Newid is a clever play on words, "Traws" is short for Trawsfynydd and "Newid" is Welsh for change. In addition "trawsnewid" is also Welsh for transform. Local 'ownership' and influence in the decision-making process are the most important components of the company. To this end, it has 137 ordinary members from the community of Trawsfynydd and is run by a board of 9 directors. The directors are answerable to, and are voted for, by the members through the annual general meeting. Traws-Newid is also very proud to have as its Honorary President Dr. John Elfed Jones, whose wisdom and contacts are priceless assets.

Then to complete the operational side of the company, we are extremely fortunate in having one of the most conscientious and dedicated managers possible in Karen Hughes, whose sterling work and no-nonsense but friendly attitude ensures that the company runs smoothly and efficiently.

I return to the development of the lake and Highgate. Starting with the lake, BNFL

Magnox, as stated above, were willing to give us the superior licence to develop the lake for tourism and leisure purposes provided that any profits gained were re-invested in the village. We had no problem with this caveat; indeed, it was part of our vision to be able to utilise local resources for the benefit of the community. This alternative revenue source would also provide environmental improvements to the streetscape that would otherwise be unattainable by the Community Council due to insufficient funds.

So how could we make money out of it? Easy, by acting as 'landlords' and charging our 'tenants' rent for the privilege of using the lake, and the land surrounding it in some instances, for canoeing, sailing, fishing, etc. Incidentally the lake has an excellent reputation for fishing, under the auspices of the Prysor Angling Association, who often play host to both national and international fishing competitions.

It was a pleasure indeed to have the company of Peter Rogers AM on the 22 May 2000, when he visited us to see our various schemes, which included the following:

The first phase of Highgate – renovating the building's outer envelope
Salem Garden – National Park award winning community garden, built on the site of a former chapel whose plot was donated to the Community Council, and cared for by volunteers
Brynglas – an off-road parking scheme, previously an extremely narrow part of the high street with parking problems which presented a hazard to pedestrians
Utica – BNFL Magnox's former district survey laboratory. Traws-Newid converted it, with grant aid, into office starter units for small or fledgling businesses.
The tour finished with a cruise on the lake aboard "Mared", a former Amsterdam waterbus operated by a local farmer, with Traws-Newid providing landing facilities in the shape of a floating pontoon for the boat.

Concerning the Highgate project, 29 August 2000, was a very important day for us when a black limousine pulled up outside the building, with its door opening for us to greet the then Assembly Secretary for Housing and Local Government, Peter Law AM. It was a very proud moment for us to guide Mr Law around what had formerly been the village Co-op store, and was now being transformed into a centre for enterprise and community development.

"A centre for what?" - let me explain. The building is a three-storey building plus a basement. It started life as a hotel, then temperance hotel, before becoming a Co-op. It is therefore a comparatively large building and it benefits from being located in the centre of the village.

Starting from the bottom, the basement has been converted into a workshop and has been let to a local craft business. The ground floor will be an interpretation centre based upon the life and times of Hedd Wyn, together with another famous person who was born near Traws, the recently rediscovered Catholic Saint and Martyr, John Roberts, who was hung, drawn and quartered at Tyburn in 1610, and is one of the Forty Martyrs of England and Wales. The second and third floor will provide bunkhouse type accommodation for cyclists, together with a manager's office. There will also be provision within the building for the community and small businesses to have access to computers, photocopier, fax machine, etc. The Assembly has already provided £97,000 towards the scheme through the European Regional Development Fund (ERDF), which it administrates. The total value of the project will be approximately £600,000.

The accommodation for cyclists referred to above brings us nicely back to the lake, or to be more precise a cycle track along the lake's shore. The 11th of October 2002 marked the official opening of a £175,000 cycle track from Traws to nearby Gellilydan by Richard Edwards AM, Chair of the Assembly's Transport, Planning and Environment Committee. Dafydd Elis-Thomas AM also attended the occasion, and it is pleasing to note that both have taken a keen interest in our schemes as well as providing support and encouragement for our various projects and activities. Attracting cyclists will no doubt help the local economy. However, not only will it be of economic benefit, the trail also passes through breathtaking mountain scenery and provides a less hazardous route for cyclists than the busy A470 trunk road that they would use otherwise. In the future it is hoped to extend this route to link up with the national mountain bike centre at Maesgwm, about five miles south of Traws, which currently attracts around 170,000 cyclists.

Traws-Newid's relationships with Richard Edwards goes back to November 2000, when his Committee visited Traws, where he gave us the highest accolade possible in a joint press release with Sue Essex AM, by describing Traws-Newid as, "a shining example of best practice in sustainable development". Subsequent to that visit, it was a great delight and honour to be invited by him to the Assembly to give a presentation upon our work and our achievements on the 14th February 2001 – our finest hour indeed.

Whilst this article finishes here, Traws-Newid's work doesn't, with further plans to develop a pilgrimage trail following the footsteps of St. John Roberts together with a Meirionnydd Christianity Trail, creating a sports ground for youngsters, redeveloping a memorial park, updating our web site www.trawsnewid.btinternet.co.uk – and the list goes on! Regenerating a community is a long-term commitment that requires dedicated people with a shared vision. Here, in Traws, we're fortunate in having such people who are willing to go that extra mile for the benefit of their community, particularly our hardworking fundraisers. That task is made so much easier by having the support and help of the Assembly, as well as the other agencies and authorities, too numerous to mention, but much appreciated!

Keith T O'Brien lives in Trawsfynydd with his wife and two daughters, aged 9 and 14 years. He is a local government officer and a Community Councillor as well as being the Chair of Traws-Newid.

Foot and Mouth

By Michael Cruchley

Rural Officer for the National Synod of Wales of The United Reformed Church and Co-ordinator of the CYTÛN Rural Network

February 2001 will stay in the minds of many people in rural Wales, as in other parts of the United Kingdom, as the start of an *annus horribilis*. When Foot and Mouth Disease was discovered and confirmed in Essex few realised that life in the countryside would be so severely disrupted for so long. Wales is a long way from Essex, so why be too worried? Yet soon the impact was felt in this country.

Closure of markets, restriction on movement and sales soon took their toll. Then other businesses started to feel the impact as people were advised not to visit the countryside unless absolutely necessary. Holidays - especially the short break holiday, the weekend away, were cancelled and changed. Instead of a visit to the countryside, city breaks became more popular. Where would the impact stop? When would the disease be controlled? "How long, O Lord, how long?" As one friend put it, "For the farming community it was just one damned thing after another!" Government handling of the situation was widely criticised as outdated and inept.

By the end of February the churches across the United Kingdom were asked to launch an appeal to assist people whose livelihood would be damaged. The ARC Addington Fund was established very quickly, with the object of helping those directly dependent upon agriculture for their living. A simple scheme was established whereby those in need could apply through a third party referee for a small grant to assist them.

To begin with the third party referees came through the churches - local ministers and members who had some knowledge of farming. The referees were all volunteers and, working with a very small staff in an office at The Arthur Rank Centre, the churches centre for rural affairs, at Stoneleigh, started to pay out grants. The members of the staff were themselves volunteers, or were seconded by other organisations. The fund raising was done almost by word of mouth - the appeal being sent through the churches initially, but - thank God - taken up by regional and national press. From the first meeting of Trustees in March 2001 when there were 10 requests for help and no money to give, to the time the giving of cash grants was stopped in June 2002, over £10.5 million had been given in approximately 24,000 grants. The Trustees decided that a maximum of four grants could be made to any one farming business. As the need increased, a small staff was employed but still mainly by secondment. Costs were kept as low as possible and administration costs have not risen above 1.5%.

What were the grants for? It soon became clear that many farmers, although not having the disease on their holdings or being affected by any contiguous cull impact, were facing serious problems because of movement restrictions. In Wales, the outbreak first occurred at lambing time when people and livestock are always under extra pressure. To be unable to trade - thereby cutting off cash flow - and to have extra stock to feed raised the pressure still further. A vicious spiral had started. For many hill farmers there was an added problem. Sheep had been sent to lower ground, 'on tack', in other parts of Wales or England. Because of movement restrictions they could not be brought home. Many were on mainly arable farms where there was little experience of livestock management, especially of lambing! Not only that, but the land was needed for its normal use as spring came. Stock in one place, farmer in another, feed to provide and rent to pay. The spiral twisted further. Before long there was a shortage of fodder and straw. In any case, due to normal market forces, the price rose for what fodder and straw was available. Extra stock, therefore extra feed and bedding, and no income = stress! With the improvement in the weather as winter turned to spring and then to summer, the stock would normally have been moved to hill pastures - but - movement was not allowed because of the risk of spreading the disease. More stock in more crowded conditions - the spiral of need and no income twisted higher. The ARC Addington referees, now joined by staff of the farming unions, accountants, retired farmers, were faced with trying to help with small amounts when the need was so high. No grant was more than £2000, yet referees became aware that the need of many farmers was for many thousands of pounds. Many were already deeply in debt because of low prices for their products and the continuing impact of BSE and bovine TB Many had seen the publication of statistics about farm incomes over the past few years, but the implications remained hidden amongst a proud and often silent people. Some farmers made visible protest, but many were found to have been quietly sinking into debt having used their savings to prop up their business. The stock's welfare was more important to them than their own.

Alongside the need in the farming community, it quickly became clear that other small businesses as well as direct farming were being harmed. Farming contractors, machinery maintenance businesses and the like were obvious sufferers. The need for veterinary service and medicine grew, but with no income farmers struggled to pay - or just could not do so. Few seemed to notice, to begin with, that local Bed and Breakfast establishments, tourism attractions (often small scale) and local gift shops were suffering too. It even went as far as the suppliers to those businesses. For instance, those supplying groceries etc., to local B and B's and small hotels lost trade. Small businesses whose main outlet was at agricultural shows found their income had sharply declined, if not stopped. It was good that ARC Addington was given money by other Trusts, primarily The Rank Foundation, specifically to help non-agricultural businesses.

So, did the need outweigh the resource? As with most questions of this sort, the answer is both "Yes" and "No".
Yes - because no one could be helped to the point whereby his or her business moved from debt to profit; his or her bank balance from deep red to healthy black!
Yes - because problems continued through the months that followed until trading could resume - and some still exist at the time of writing almost two years on from the outbreak!
No - because few requests were turned down. Of course some would have liked more but the resource had to be shared as equably as possible.
No - because conversations were begun and have continued between referees and applicants.
A sense of support and friendship had been established that helped relieve some of the stress that developed. The fund staff and many referees received letters expressing real thanks for the money but even more for the sense of support and care offered it represented.

The ARC Addington Fund was not alone in this work. The Royal Agricultural Benevolent Institution (RABI) was working harder than ever to help farming families struggling to meet domestic bills at a time of little income. It has been interesting to see that both funds have been able to make roughly similar amounts of money available to those in need. In some parts of Wales new support groups have been established. Whilst not having cash to give away, they offer the emotional support of friendship and understanding proven to be vital. Telephone help lines were opened and widely used by people at the end of their tether.

The work was not without its critics. There are those who consider farming to be "feather-bedded" by subsidy and who question whether farming and rural businesses were more deserving during the outbreak than those who suffered job-losses in the decline of the mining and steel industries. In each and every case of industrial decline where people's livelihood is harmed there is cause for real concern. The work of the 'rural' charities in 2001 and 2002 was not trying to say that their recipients were more deserving than others, but that they were in need. Many farms and rural businesses lost not only income but capital asset as well, for home and business is often tied together for them.

Since this is a book about the way in which the 'political' world has touched the 'real' one, what about the role of the National Assembly in all of this? Was it a case of "Foot in Mouth"? Whether there should be a greater devolution of responsibility for Agriculture and Rural Affairs is not under discussion here, although in the light of experience the ability to make decisions about Wales and Foot and Mouth Disease at a more local level would probably have been helpful. Experience suggests that the principle of subsidiarity could bear further examination.

Early in the outbreak, Her Majesty's Government in Westminster promised to "match fund" public donation to funds such as ARC Addington. The National Assembly accepted that it should do the same, though with much less funding available to it. Ministers and civil servants alike were anxious to help and did their utmost, I believe. Everyone is aware that there is never as much help available as some believe is needed! Yet ARC Addington received close to £1.95million from the Assembly in match funding. 7362 grants were made in Wales, totalling just under £3.5million. ARC Addington grants were made to assist the establishment or expansion of other support services.

RABI also gave and received in the same way - a total of £2.4 million special Foot and Mouth Disease support was given between 1st March 2001 and 31st August 2002 to 1846 farming families (some had more than one grant). This was in addition to its regular support of over £500,000 to Welsh farmers in the same period. The match funding from the National Assembly for RABI came to close to £50,000. The Wales Rural Stress Helpline extended both its times of availability and geographic spread to cover the whole country.

At the same time a Task and Finish Group was established by the Assembly to assist in the preparation of a Rural Recovery Plan. CYTÛN (Churches Together in Wales) was invited to be part of the secretariat of that Task Group and was asked to offer a paper on the human cost of Foot and Mouth Disease. Whilst the Recovery Plan did not include a specific section on the human costs, there were indications at many points of the awareness of personal hardship and distress that the paper had addressed. Money was made available to further support those working to alleviate stress in rural communities and for the provision of four new mental health workers in those areas most affected by Foot and Mouth Disease.

As mentioned earlier, criticism can always be made about "not enough" or "not quickly enough" (Too little, too late!). Yet I reflect that Assembly staff tried to help within the limits of their responsibilities - and they still want to see support being given where there is proven need. Wales did not have as many cases of Foot and Mouth Disease as other parts of the UK, but the needs exposed as a result of the disease tell of the struggling state of the rural economy in Wales prior to the outbreak. It can be said that much was done, but there is even more still to be done if rural Wales is to make the most of its greatest resource - its people - who care for the beautiful land.

Thank you - National Assembly and people of Wales - for your concern and support, but do not forget or ignore our rural people and businesses now!

The Revd Michael Cruchley is the Rural Officer for the National Synod of Wales of The United Reformed Church and is the co-ordinator of the CYTÛN Rural Network. He is a Trustee of the ARC Addington Fund on behalf of the churches of Wales.

Confronting a Welsh Not

By Aled Edwards

Faith Communities Representative on the National Assembly's Voluntary Sector Partnership Council

Few National Assembly press releases have given me more personal satisfaction than the statement issued on Saint Valentine's Day, 2003. I had been contacted by the Assembly press office on the previous Wednesday to provide a quote welcoming the news that the Criminal Records Bureau (CRB), after a long and monumental struggle, had agreed to produce a set of Welsh language forms for their 'Disclosure' service. It gave me great pleasure to welcome the announcement.

I have dealt with more important issues at the Assembly, but getting the Liverpool based CRB to abide by the principle of equality between Wales' two primary languages, as intended in the *1993 Welsh Language Act,* had become a personal as well as a professional struggle. I am, after all, a first language Welsh speaker who wishes to live his life, as far as possible, through the medium of his own language. Beyond that, I hate being expected to collude with the less than adequate rhetoric of large bureaucracies. The CRB, had after all, been given the onerous responsibility by the state of administering adequately the checks on individuals who came in contact with vulnerable people. Capita, the private company servicing the CRB was also expected to make a considerable amount of money out of this private – public arrangement. It was openly stated by the CRB that the contract could be worth £400 million over a ten year period. Given that fiscal reality, Welsh-speakers should never have been asked to accept a less than equal linguistic provision or be encouraged by an executive arm of the Home Office to make a choice, as crude 'customers' in a social market place, to chose between protecting the vulnerable and being able to use their own language.

My first political engagement over the CRB was, strangely, a positive experience. With fellow members of the Assembly's Voluntary Sector Partnership Council (VSPC), I had pressed the case for the Home Office to waive the fee for checks on volunteers who came into contact with children and other vulnerable groups. The Council meets about four times a year and brings together Assembly Members, key officials from the civil service and twenty one representatives from the voluntary sector. We had protested that having to pay the full fees for checks on volunteers could cost millions and possibly threatened the well being of the vulnerable people the original legislation had been designed to protect. The sheer cost could have, for example, brought several sports activities involving Wales' children and young people to a halt and even threatened some crucial volunteer services to the elderly. Quietly and to great effect, Jane Hutt, the Assembly's Health and Social Services Minister, brought our protest to the attention of the Home Office. It was announced in February, 2001, much to our relief, that checks would be free of charge for volunteers.

My next political involvement with the CRB began in earnest at the Denbigh National

Eisteddfod seven months later. Several churches and a number of voluntary groups such as *Urdd Gobaith Cymru* (The Welsh League of Youth) had indicated that they expected the CRB to provide Welsh language forms particularly for its Enhanced and Standard Disclosure Service. I can remember walking over to the Welsh Language Board's tent with a colleague to indicate our concern that no Welsh forms, to date, had been provided and that they would be needed once the CRB's service was fully on line. Assurances were given that the Board was in constant contact with the CRB and that our concerns would be duly recorded. The Welsh Language Board staff kept their word and continued over many months, but to no apparent avail, to make the appropriate representations to the CRB.

To his credit, early in 2002, Bernard Herdan, the CRB's Chief Executive actually visited the National Assembly with members of his team. For me, the experience remains memorable. The visit provided voluntary and faith groups with the opportunity to assure the CRB of their commitment to protecting the vulnerable, but to state clearly that some would also require Welsh language application forms. I was not convinced at the time that the CRB understood that Welsh speakers ask for services in their own language not because of an inability to understand English, but because of a desire to live daily lives, as far as possible, through the medium of Welsh. I distinctly remember not responding well to receiving a glossy Welsh booklet to help me understand the English only application forms or to being reminded that looking after the vulnerable was more important than protecting the language. I never doubted or questioned that particular priority. I just believed, in the context of such a substantial public-private partnership contract, that the CRB could well afford to protect the vulnerable and respect the rights of Welsh speakers.

What followed, provided me with a vivid example of why people, when confronting large and obstinate institutions, find the need to protest rather than to engage in a process. Even large public bodies and national legislatures can find themselves at the receiving end of crude political obstinacy from larger powers. Having failed at that time, in the company of the Welsh Language Board and the National Assembly, to persuade the CRB to provide a Welsh language service on an equal basis with the English provision, it was decided, in July 2002, to convey the frustrations of some faith communities by writing directly to the Home Office. The CRB is an Executive Agency of the Home Office. They, with moronic monotony, passed the letter back to the CRB.

The response gained from the CRB arrived in early September. Bernard Herdan gave the obtuse assurance that the Bureau recognised the 'importance of allowing its customers to deal with the Bureau in their chosen language' and that it was 'fully committed to the principles set out in the Welsh Language Act 1993'. However, it was also stated that Standard and Enhanced Disclosure application forms would be produced only at the stage the CRB perceived to be the 'earliest practicable opportunity' – several months after the publication of the English only application forms. The letter explained further that the Bureau was not persuaded that 'it should introduce similar arrangements for Registration and Countersignatory application forms.' This meant that major Welsh bodies, who wanted to do so, could not register with the CRB by means of a Welsh language application form. The CRB had decided, in the specific context of their provision of Welsh language application forms for Registration and Countersignatory, to practice a 'Welsh not' policy.

Around the periphery of the issue the Bureau had made some provision for Welsh speakers by placing a few Welsh pages on its internet site and by employing some Welsh speakers who could 'deal with' Welsh correspondence and callers on their helpline. The closing paragraph of Bernard Herdan's September 2002 letter is worth quoting in full:

> I hope that you will accept that the interim measures that the Bureau has introduced go a long way to meeting the expectations of its customers in Wales. And, given the primary role of the CRB Disclosure service in protecting children and vulnerable members of society, that you will encourage all Welsh-speaking customers who wish to register with the CRB or to apply for Disclosure to do so on existing forms. While these forms are currently available in English only, they can still be completed in Welsh and guidance on their completion is already available in Welsh.

The CRB had learnt little during or since their visit to the National Assembly. Apparently, Welsh-speakers still needed a lesson in priority setting where it came to protecting the vulnerable and some further, but limited help was deemed necessary and reasonable, to help access the Bureau's English only application forms. It was crystal clear that engaging with the CRB as a 'power' would demand both protest and process.

My personal understanding, as a Christian priest, of how 'powers' such as the CRB work is heavily influenced by theology. The American theologian Walter Wink, in *The Powers That Be* (1998), provides a Christian model for understanding how good and evil forces operate in the modern world through 'powers'. The 'powers', to follow Wink's analysis, may be departments of government, councils, companies, quangos, voluntary groups or bodies such as the CRB and the National Assembly. He goes beyond the issue of how power is used to explore the nature of the 'powers' themselves and explored an integral worldview of reality which sees everything as having an outer and an inner aspect – both physical and spiritual.

Wink explains vividly that all of us encounter 'powers'. To contextualise it bluntly, in Wales, they staff our schools and hospitals, they run County Hall, the National Assembly and the Houses of Parliament, they sit in corporate boardrooms, collect taxes, foster political parties and head families. 'Powers', however, are more than people. As systems they weave society into an intricate fabric of power and relationships. They surround us on all sides and are necessary and useful. They employ people who enjoy their jobs. They make a genuine contribution to our society. They also do good. Sometimes, however, they are the sources of unmitigated evils. Often they do good and evil at the same time. The CRB is a 'power' like all other 'powers'. Its refusal to produce Welsh language application forms flowed from both its corporate and market based culture and its collective personality. Sadly, it could almost be said that no-one should have been surprised, given its cultural packaging, that the Bureau should have behaved in any other way.

Wink quite rightly states that 'powers' such as the CRB have to be confronted primarily by being 'named'. In politics, real power over the less powerful is frequently exercised by those who prefer not be 'named'. In the case of the CRB's stance over the Welsh language, the 'naming' was done relentlessly through the Welsh press and media during the summer of 2002. Questions were also asked at the Saint David's National Eisteddfod during open debates on the future of the Welsh language at the Assembly's stand. The Eisteddfod session was followed up by articles in the *Western Mail*. It should also be noted, that in terms of the dialogue between the different faces of government departments and agencies, the Welsh Language Board quietly placed its own distinctive 'naming' ignominy upon the CRB by refusing to accept its draft language scheme. The Bureau was told that its draft scheme would not be accepted until it rectified its approach to the provision of Welsh language material.

Further 'naming' was achieved through *Radio Cymru* and the BBC's Welsh language internet service *Cymru'r Byd* during August and September when much sharper rods were being placed on the CRB's rather raw back over questions such as checking new teachers. The Bureau had an England and Wales wide crisis on its hands. During such heated days, one could have given the CRB a break on the language front, but political 'naming' is not an exercise to be toyed with by the weak willed. The Bureau should have provided an equal linguistic provision a year before. They were an Eisteddfod too late to be granted generosity.

Protest however, was never going to be enough. The protests would have to be taken through a political process. During May 2002, following a robust conversation over the CRB at the VSPC meeting in Merthyr, Jane Hutt, the Assembly's Minister for Health and Social Services agreed to establish a Working Group consisting of key Assembly officials and voluntary sector members on the Council, namely myself (Faith Communities), Graham Benfield (WCVA) , Keith Dunn (St John's Ambulance Brigade, Wales), Catrin Fletcher (Volunteering), Veronica Wilson (Youth), Catriona Williams (Children and Families); Sue Pickavance (Director of the WCVA's Volunteering Unit) and Jim Crowe (SCOVO) with the following terms of reference:

- to assess the annual costs to the voluntary sector in Wales of the administration, preparation and submission of disclosure applications to the Criminal Records Bureau;
- to consider how an efficient and cost-effective service for the administration of disclosure applications might be delivered to the voluntary sector and to make recommendations; and
- to review the Criminal Record Bureau's operational policy in relation to the Welsh language, to consider its appropriateness and to make recommendations.

Such processes, although largely unnoticed by the public, represent a radically new and effective way of doing politics in Wales. The Voluntary Sector Partnership Council, although hard work at times, is far more than a talking shop. Through the CRB Working Group, leaders from Wales' voluntary world were brought into a common process with each other, and with key members of staff from the Welsh Language Board and the Welsh Assembly Government. All worked together, from very different perspectives and responsibilities, to achieve a common goal. It is to be regretted that, all too often, the creative and enabling stories brought about by such processes rarely become part of a nation's shared narrative.

During its first formal meeting in September, 2002, the Working Group drew a line that, come what may, would not be crossed over the language issue. The CRB's policy was simply unacceptable. From then on, it took more than one correspondence between the Assembly's First Minister and the Home Office and further letters from other players to 'deal with' the Bureau's 'Welsh not'.

By the full meeting of the Voluntary Sector Partnership Council held on Valentine's Day, 2003, at the Newport Centre, the Working Group could rejoice in the announcement that the CRB had changed its policy on the Welsh language. It had also gathered together important data on the financial implications of performing Standard and Enhanced checks on volunteers. Crucially, it presented a formal recommendation that a new National Assembly sponsored umbrella body should be set up in Wales to help process checks on volunteers. The recommendation gained the support of all the members of the Voluntary Sector Partnership Council including the political parties. It was announced recently that such a body will be set up by September 2003 with Assembly funding.

The National Assembly and the Art of Conversation

By David Melding
Conservative Assembly Member South Wales Central

The Conservative philosopher Michael Oakeshott considered language, or more precisely conversation, to be the most enduring metaphor of the human condition. Our world is a world of response. This is the immanent miracle of creation. Oakeshott identified several modes of speech for analysis, including those of practical activity (the realm of politics), science, religion, and history. But the greatest was, to use the title of his most sublime essay, "The Voice of Poetry in the Conversation of Mankind". When these modes of speech engage each other in conversation, the world is seen to be more coherent. Discord results when conversation descends into argument, an obvious example being the clash between science and religion in modern thought. One of the reasons (there were many) Oakeshott disliked party politics was the habitual use of corrosive argument by politicians. As he observed: "Conversation is not an enterprise designed to yield an extrinsic profit, a contest where a winner gets a prize, nor is it an activity of exegesis; it is an unrehearsed intellectual adventure". It seems to me fair to examine whether the National Assembly is more than its government and ask if Wales has become a more eloquent political entity since devolution.

Like Edmund Burke before him, Oakeshott saw a profound unity existing between generations in a moral association which is, 'unavoidably concerned with the young and the old, with those who are setting out and with those who are making the difficult exchange of hope for faith, with men and with women, with those who are born to die young and those who live into old age'. Moral association, the civil condition, is an end in itself; there is no extrinsic purpose or enterprise, only a framework within which citizens pursue their various interests. The civil condition cannot be confused, for instance, with goals such as the promotion of social welfare. It might be the case that social welfare is a worthy pursuit within the civil condition (this is a view firmly rooted in the Christian tradition). But without a coherent civil association, such pursuits can never be authentically advanced. This is why many Conservatives did not see devolution as the automatic route to better public policies, but as a new set of responsibilities which could lead to good or bad outcomes depending on the quality of political decision-making within the Assembly.

The National Assembly was the product of much argument and a little conversation. It is now the visible evidence of a great truth: Wales has become a political nation. We can no longer limit Welshness to a cultural identity (although it remains that in part). A much stronger civil association exists in Wales and we must all learn to converse with each other more clearly. I can hear the popular refrain "All they do is talk, talk, talk!" But do we talk well in the National Assembly, or are ours "the babblings of men who speak, but do not speak the same language" (Oakeshott again). It is only through coherent conversation that sound policies can be adduced and tested by reasonable scrutiny. And it is not only AMs who are responsible for this political discourse within the Assembly, but rather the whole of society. The electorate is not struck mute by the act of voting.

The result of coherent conversation is not 'consensus politics', at least not as that rum notion is usually understood. To the politically elect, 'consensus politics' means the acceptance by the lost of their fallen state. Here the politically lost gain redemption by acquiescence to the general will (the Holy Ghost of rationalist thought). It is not merely bad manners for the lost to question the victor's manifesto, it is positively wicked. Not only must party X accept that party Y won, it must repent and greet the victor's gospel. I would suggest an alternative definition of 'consensus politics'. It should be a political process that encourages the art of conversation and allows political parties to agree when they agree (at least half of the time) and disagree when points of difference genuinely exist. It is the 'game' element of politics that puts many people off and is driving down turnout at elections. The electorate is too sophisticated to be fooled by feigned arguments and pretended differences. When political parties concentrate on authentic points of disagreement, they sharpen political discourse and present real alternatives to the electorate. This can be done without damaging the stock of policies that behind the scenes receive all-party support. I would say that the National Assembly has made some limited progress in promoting a more coherent political discourse.

The voices of all four major political parties are heard loud and clear in the Assembly. This was not inevitable. The Assembly could have become a monologue for the Labour Party. We can thank Ron Davies for anticipating just how destructive such a soliloquy would have been in a fledging institution.

The regional list system ensured that there was a Conservative group of nine members, not one or two, for instance. Acts of grace by governing parties are very rare indeed; the Labour Party deserves sincere praise for the decision to use an element of Proportional Representation in the Assembly's elections. Not only has this resulted in an Assembly that reflects the major strands of political thought in Wales, it has helped the Conservative Party accept the immutability of devolution in all foreseeable circumstances short of constitutional breakdown. To have left the Conservative Party without an effective voice would have damaged both the Assembly and the emerging Welsh Conservative Party.

If Proportional Representation has ensured that the Assembly is a benign and ever harmonious Tower of Babel (with a translation unit thrown in), the internal business of the institution has been shaped by another act of political generosity. The Business Committee is made up of one member from each political party represented in the Assembly. So the dark and deep currents of the usual channels do not run through the Assembly, but a more pellucid process determines the political agenda. The coalition government remains by far the strongest force, but the voices of the minority parties cannot be silenced. It should be noted that very little disruption has occurred in the Assembly and all parties have been content to avoid obstruction and spoiling tactics. Although I dislike the phrase, the label 'inclusive politics' has some validity in describing the conduct of Assembly business. The same can be said of the public appointments process which has been considerably improved by the inclusion of representatives from each party on the selection panels.

I have concentrated on processes rather than outcomes. However, in many of the Assembly's actions the voice of authentic consensus can be heard. *The Waterhouse Report* made the most unspeakable darkness visible. Those who read the report were deeply affected by the catalogue of abuse inflicted on some of the most vulnerable children in society. The words of St. Matthew ring true "But whoso shall offend one of these little ones which believe in me, it were better for him that a millstone were hanged about his neck, and that he were drowned in the depth of the sea" (18.6). Yet such indignation can be a self-serving attempt to atone for past silence. Those in care did speak, but on the rare occasions they were heard, they were not believed. Now all children in Wales have a voice in the form of a Children's Commissioner, the first in the UK. Devolution has allowed us in Wales to make an articulate response to a grave crisis. It is to be hoped that the all-party consensus that called for a Children's Commissioner represents an acceptance that social care should be at the top of the political agenda. The Health and Social Services Committee worked in close collaboration with the Minister and helped shape policy. Generally speaking, the Committee sought to make the post of Children's Commissioner as independent as possible and the Minister accepted the need for complete impartiality. Although the Assembly appoints the Commissioner, the term is a long one (seven years) and cannot be extended or repeated. This ensures that the Commissioner does not have one eye on reappointment. There is no incentive to pull punches. The appointment process also broke new ground. Probably for the first time anywhere, young people were central to the process and sat on the selection panel. A special representative conference was also held where young people interviewed all of the applicants for the post of Commissioner and then made a report to the selection panel (both the conference and the selection panel reached the same conclusion). The Assembly is rightly proud of this innovation, even if it was born of the most dreadful necessity.

Conversation can get too cosy. It needs some edge to be stimulating. Those of us who represent minority parties must occasionally answer back in civil tones. Political options exist in all mature democracies and it is the duty of minority parties to present alternative programmes of government. The 2003 Assembly elections will test the robustness of both Plaid Cymru and the Welsh Conservative Party in this respect. The election manifestos will be a key test to determine whether the political parties can speak clearly to the Welsh electorate. Any manifesto that is a mere wish list will surely be greeted with derision. If several coherent programmes for government are offered to the Welsh electorate, then the quality of political conversation will be high. The National Assembly would have succeeded in strengthening political parties in Wales; and this would be good for the future health of a new-born political nation.

Public attitudes to the National Assembly are wise and instructive. A clear (and growing) majority accept devolution. The fact that Wales is now a political nation is broadly welcomed. Assembly Members seem closer to the people they represent, and access to decision-makers is easier. More scepticism is expressed about the particular actions of the Assembly's government. This is the most encouraging indication of health in our new body politic. A clear distinction is being made between the Assembly and the Assembly's government (still constitutionally Siamese twins, but formal separation is inevitable). The National Assembly has gained a high level of acceptance and therefore legitimacy. I would regard this as a commonplace observation, but this outcome was in no way assured. There is a rock lurking beneath these calm constitutional waters. Turnout in the second round of Assembly elections is predicted to be very low. Nevertheless, turnout is only one measure of political participation. There is ample evidence of the success of consultation exercises between the Assembly and the public and sectors like business and voluntary organisations. The Assembly has a Voluntary Sector Partnership Council (and there are Councils for Local Government and the Business Sector). Regional Committees meet in every part of Wales and hold "open microphone" sessions to allow the public to question AMs and ministers. In these forums, which are still underdeveloped, conversation is risky and cannot be easily anticipated or controlled by the government.

The art of conversation is key to the success of any free political association. Good conversation leads to sound judgement and the likelihood of successful policy decisions. When conversation is coherent, many voices mingle, some grow fainter others stronger, and the tenses of many generations are present. According to Hobbes, without speech and conversation there can be no "commonwealth nor society nor contract nor peace". Political conversation must be open to all and never made the preserve of politicians. Conversation is not true or false (as arguments claim to be) but more or less coherent, clear or confused, delightful or dull. The people of Wales are yet to decide whether they think the Assembly delightful or dull, but they want to continue the conversation.

David Melding was born in 1962. He was educated in Cardiff and Virginia, USA. He was the Manager of the Carers National Association in Wales and is a former Deputy Director of the Welsh Centre for International Affairs. He is the Welsh Conservative Party's spokesperson on health and social services. His interests include community care and health.

From the Cradle to The Bus Pass

The Hundreds and Thousands Stories

By Aled Edwards

Thus far, by telling stories, this book has sought to provide a platform by which some important Assembly stories can be highlighted in the public domain. They have, on the whole, flowed from the endeavours of individuals who have engaged successfully with a new political process and institution on behalf of communities, specific interest groups and sectors. There will no doubt be, from other backgrounds and opinions, more stories and storytellers.

In this closing chapter, I will try to bridge a rather wide gap by publishing an updated personal record of 'devolution differences' that have been brought about for the many. Regardless perhaps of public perception, it would be difficult, by now, to find anyone in Wales whose life has not been impacted upon, in one way or another, by decisions taken at the Assembly. Such rare creatures amongst Wales' 2.9 million people would have had to avoid all local government services, schools, colleges, surgeries, hospitals, roads, many cultural and sporting events, national museums and several places of work.

The record also looks beyond Wales. It shows how the Welsh Assembly Government's actions have made a difference to the lives of millions who live in other parts of the United Kingdom - especially deprived areas, disenfranchised groups and Welsh speaking communities in distant places such as Patagonia in Argentina. The breadth of Wales' contribution to the worldwide sustainable development debate is also noted.

It has to be conceded at the outset that ascertaining genuine differences in the context of the National Assembly has been no easy task. The Assembly is not a stand-alone political institution. The record therefore, highlights issues where the Assembly has made an important or decisive difference. It will have made a difference alongside other agencies and political institutions.

It is also conceded that doing things differently in Wales is not an entirely new phenomenon. Following the formation of the Welsh Office in 1964, Wales did at times plough its own furrow. However, differences tended to emerge in reaction to UK policies rather than from indigenous policy formation. It should be noted that, beyond Welsh language related legislation and regulations of a local nature such as traffic orders, Lord Gwilym Prys Davies (2000), in his Llanelli Eisteddfod Law Society Lecture, questioned whether more than around 120 separate pieces of subordinate legislation had been passed by the Welsh Office from 1964 to 1999. The Welsh Office may have ploughed its own furrow, but it did so within certain confines. This has changed.

For the sake of simplicity, my record tends to discuss the National Assembly as a body corporate. Such a simplicity may well be accurate in law since the Assembly was created as a body corporate, but it may be misleading as regards the daily reality of Welsh politics. The National Assembly for Wales and the so named *Welsh Assembly Government,* as the executive, are not synonymous. The Welsh Assembly Government may have delivered most of the differences specified in my list, but the changes sometimes represent variations brought about by political processes reflecting the breadth of the Assembly's activities and representations. They are therefore fairly regarded as 'devolution differences'. These include the partnership document between Labour and the Liberal Democrats, and a far more vibrant political engagement on the part of key sectors in Welsh civic society through bodies such as the Voluntary Sector Partnership Council.

In an attempt to discern genuine differences of importance to people, I have limited references to political processes such as target setting, the publication of strategies and announcing small percentage increases in UK government expenditure as it has filtered through to Wales. The differences included in the record flow from five distinct sources:

(a) Changes specifically brought about by the *Government of Wales Act 1998.*
(b) Changes brought about by the internal processes of the National Assembly such as the work of the subject committees and the partnership councils, greater political scrutiny, and coalition government.
(c) Distinct Welsh policies initiated or developed since devolution by the Welsh Assembly Government.
(d) The capacity of the National Assembly to lobby for Wales in a way which UK cabinet protocols would not allow a Secretary of State for Wales.
(e) A more Wales based focus on behalf of civic society following devolution.

The list does include, for example, some changes to draft Assembly budgets following public consultations and recommendations from the subject committees. Such changes, as small as they may be, would not have occurred in Wales prior to the formation of the National Assembly.

The other UK legislatures have, between them, introduced unique policies to England, Scotland and Northern Ireland. The following list does not attempt to assess the comparative effectiveness or value of the variations or to list the Welsh Assembly Government's 'sins of omission'. It merely seeks to state some of the differences brought about by Welsh devolution.

The 'Top Twenty' differences are mine in terms of priority. I readily accept that not everyone would share my taste in priorities. It matters not. All the other differences have been placed in chronological order according to reference dates.

Top 20 Differences

Political Accountability - Placed control over an annual budget of some £11 billion and the passing of several forms of legislation affecting over 2.9 million people, in the hands of elected representatives directly accountable to the people of Wales. Over a million people voted in the Welsh Assembly Elections on 6 May 1999.

Open Government – Provided Wales with one of the most open legislatures in the world through the early publication of cabinet papers, open subject, regional and audit committees, statutory partnership councils and the use of modern information technology. The Assembly also insists, for example, upon cross party involvement for all public appointments in Wales for which Assembly subject committees have oversight and that no public appointment should be made by an Assembly Minister without the involvement an independent assessor.

Setting Welsh Financial Priorities – Set a Draft Welsh Budget for the period 2002/03 to 2005/06 by allocating an additional: 18% for health and Social Services, 16% for local government, 66% for communities, 14% for environment and planning, 14% for Agriculture and Rural Affairs, 8% for economic development, 29% for education and 44% for culture and sport. The apparent fall of –8% for Housing seems to be due to moving budget lines between expenditure groups, in particular to the new 'Communities' heading (Plenary Draft Budget November 2002).

The Economy – Successfully pressed the case for Wales' most deprived areas, over and above the population based Barnett formula, to receive a European Grants transfer of £421 million from the UK Treasury towards drawing down Objective One money worth some £1.2 billion. By admitting the principle of additionality to Wales, the Treasury conceded for the first time that there should be a 'needs based' augmentation to the Barnett Block. It was announced in December 2002 that 759 projects in West Wales and the Valleys had been given the green light and were sharing over £426 million in European grant aid (Hansard 18 July 2000).

Children – Secured an amendment to the *Care Standards Bill* establishing an Independent Children's Commissioner for Wales. It was reported in October 2002, in a survey undertaken by UNICEF, that more than 90% of children in England want a commissioner to fight for their rights. Scotland and Northern Ireland are actively considering making a similar appointment.

Young People and Life Long Learning - Announced a new Assembly Learning Grant for some 43,000 students in Higher and Further Education. £44m was made available to fund this scheme in 2002/2003 (Press Release 12 June 2002).

Pensioners - Introduced free bus travel for pensioners and disabled people in Wales. It was announced in November 2002 that almost 390,000 pensioners and disabled people were enjoying the benefits of the free bus travel (Press Release 20 November 2002).

Health - Provided vulnerable people who are assessed as needing community care with six weeks of free home care following discharge from hospital or other care (Press Release 13 March 2002).

Sustainable Development – The *Government of Wales Act 1998* gave the Assembly a legal duty to promote sustainable development - which means that the Welsh Assembly Government must govern in a way that simultaneously benefits the society, the environment and economy of Wales. This has resulted in a new style of policy development. Differences have flowed from this commitment. *The Countryside and Rights of Way Act 2000*, required the National Assembly to produce a list of the living organisms and types of habitats which are of principle importance for conserving biological diversity. The Assembly took the view that there were species and habitats that held particular significance in Wales, over and above the lists produced for England. This means that as well as species which are declining or threatened on a UK basis, Wales has included species which were once common in Wales but are now disappearing such as the lapwing and the curlew. The Welsh list recognises the importance of protecting wildlife and special wildlife places, but also takes forward the challenge to reverse the declines in our biodiversity and seek to bring back the species of plants and animals that we have lost from our wildlife in recent years.

Education - Shaped a pioneering Council for Education and Training in Wales (ELWA) with a strong regional presence and reflecting the needs of Welsh medium education and training.

The Welsh Language – Launched, with the backing of an additional £26.8 million, an *Action Plan for a Bilingual Wales*, Iaith Pawb, setting out the actions and commitments of the Assembly Government in creating a bilingual Wales (Press Release 27 November 2002).

Equal Opportunities - Resulted in the people of Wales acquiring the right to challenge by judicial review any failure to comply with equality duty including the realm of public service provision.

Local Environment - Initiated the investigation that hastened the closure of the Nantygwyddon landfill site in the Rhondda. The *Nantygwyddon Report* abandoned the standard practice of the UK National Audit Office of negotiating draft texts with the named bodies. It was announced in November 2002 that World experts on environmental health issues would visit Wales to provide advice on how the Assembly, its partners and the local community might best take forward the health-related recommendations of the Nantygwyddon Investigation (Press Release 4 November 2002).

Agriculture - Launched Farming Connect, a new system of information, advice and training to help farmers adapt their businesses. It provides a distinctively Welsh initiative which is more comprehensive and better funded than equivalent work in England. The current budget is £21 million and over 5,000 farmers have so far taken advantage of the service (Press Release 17 September 2001).

Culture and Sport - Provided free entry to museums in Wales from April 2001. It was announced in September 2002, that the policy had led to a huge increase in visitor numbers to the National Museum sites with numbers rising in the first full year of operation by 87% (Press Release 18 September 2002)

International Profile - Allowed Wales a place in the Commonwealth Parliamentary Association, which promotes democratic practices among its 54 member states.

Human Rights - Successfully lobbied for the early removal of asylum detainees from Cardiff Prison in November 2001.

Responding Better to Crises and Potential Crises – It is clear that the National Assembly has been able to offer a distinctive and more appropriate response to crises such as the *Waterhouse Report* into child abuse in north Wales, the withdrawal of the Children's Society, Foot and Mouth Disease, the Corus job losses in the steel producing communities and difficulties concerning the Criminal Records Bureau. Claims came from some of the English Regions that the Department of Trade and Industry (DTI) had not responded to the Corus job losses in a way that was either as generous or as comprehensive 'in terms of its scope' as that of the Assembly. (Peter Slater (2002) *Time for a New Regeneration Perspective*, Bevan Foundation Review 2002, page 14).

Local Government – Implemented a new approach to funding local government in Wales based on need, the clear principle that local spending choices must be paramount and that 'ringfencing' budgets for specific services is not the way forward. This should allow local authorities to respond to the key issues locally. This was backed by 15 national policy agreements, which all 22 unitary authorities have signed up for. These will tackle agreed targets between the Assembly and Local government on matters such as reductions on the class sizes, on shifting more use of public transport and on ensuring more waste recycling will ensure that key policy issues are meet and that local authorities will get additional money if the targets are met.

Making Welsh Law – Ensured, for the first time ever during 2001, that 35% of the Assembly 230 pieces of general subordinate legislation were either unique to Wales or reflected significant differences in drafting recognising Welsh circumstances (*Doing Business With The Assembly: Defining the Parameters and Utilising The Opportunities* by Winston Roddick QC). It should however be recognised that several pieces of subordinate legislation effecting Wales are still passed at Whitehall.

Some Other Differences

Children and Young People

- Announced new and uniquely Welsh set of proposals for a Foundation Phase for 3-7 year olds. The Welsh Assembly Government intends to work with experts to develop a curriculum for a new Welsh Foundation Phase from the ages of 3-7 which offers a broad range of experiences and has a positive long term effect on children's social and intellectual development (Press Release 12 February 2003).
- Announced a boost of nearly £1.3m to support the development of football in Wales for young people. The money, which will be made available over a three-year period, will be based upon the recommendations put forward by the Football Forum (Press Release 12 November 2002).
- Launched the Funky Dragon – the Children and Young People's Assembly (Press Release 12 November 2002).
- Provided a platform for the Children's Commissioner for Wales to highlight the fact that one third of all Welsh children live in poverty and what children say about poverty (Health and Social Services Committee Minutes 28 November 2002).
- Welcomed the appointment of four development officers to work with the

National Assembly to take forward a number of initiatives concerning special educational needs (Press Release 20 September 2002).

- Passed legislation making it illegal for carers to smack infants in their care (*Childminding and Day Care (Wales) Regulations 2002* came into force on 1 April 2002).
- Reimbursed local authorities in Wales for expenditure in taking care of unaccompanied asylum-seeking children (Press Release 15 January 2002).
- Welcomed the launch of the first *Special Educational Needs Code of Practice for Wales* (Press Release 18 December 2001).
- Put together a *Childcare Action Plan,* which has increased funding to local childcare partnerships and given start-up grants to childminders (Press Release 21 November 2001).
- Quickly established a task force to help sustain, until March 2003, the Children's Society advocacy and anti-poverty activity in Wales (Press Release 8 November 2001).
- Announced that the Key Stage 1 tests and tasks for seven year olds should be scrapped with immediate effect (Press Release 1 November 2001).
- Moved to establish a Special Educational Needs Tribunal for Wales (Press Release 5 September 2001).
- Pioneered legislation requiring the Children's Commissioner for Wales to have regard to the United Nations Convention on the Rights of the Child (Press Release 26 June 2001).
- Announced extra support of £150,000 for Wales's youth movement, *Urdd Gobaith Cymru* following the foot and mouth crisis (Press Release 28 April 2001).
- Created a Cabinet Sub-Committee, with published minutes, on Children and Young People (First Meeting 9 April 2001).
- Provided free school milk for nursery and primary school children (Press Release 1 February 2001).
- Provided free prescriptions for 16 to 25 year olds from April 2001 (Plenary 19 October 2000).
- Announced new funding for Early Years provision for three year olds (Plenary 19 October 2000).
- Announced an additional £1 million to improve play facilities for children (Press Release 9 May 2000).
- Created Young Voice as a forum for children and young people (Press Release 6 December 1999).
- Provided Meningitis C vaccinations for all children and young people (Press Release 1 November 1999).
- Opposed proposals, following the publication of *New Arrangements for Young People Living in and Leaving Care,* to withdraw benefits from young people aged 16-18 who leave care (Health and Social Services Committee Minutes 22 September 1999).
- Provided free dental checks for under 25s.

Life Long Learning

- Led the way in the UK by bringing back Individual Learning Accounts (ILAs). The original scheme attracted interest from over 80,000 individuals with more than 44,000 going on to use their ILA to fund learning of their choice (Press Release 26 February 2003).

- Announced £600,000 for 2001-02 to begin work on the Welsh Baccalaureate (Press Release 29 November 2000) and named the schools and colleges, which will pilot the distinctive Welsh Baccalaureate Qualification as the first ever distinctive programme for 16-19 year olds in Wales (Press Release 27 November 2002).
- Announced funding to ensure that every secondary school in Wales would receive an Intel Computer Microscope as well as the new interactive white boards (Press Release 12 November 2001).
- Published the paving document *The Learning Country* which rejects specialists schools and a significant increase in faith schools, and reaffirms a commitment to the ethos of the comprehensive system (Press Release 5 September 2001).
- Scrapped secondary school league tables (Press Release 20 July 2001).
- Raised the age limit for Modern Apprenticeships beyond 25 (Press Release 28 June 2001).
- Announced a new Skills Development Fund making half a million pounds available to support innovative projects (Press Release 28 June 2001).
- Announced the setting up set up of the new Modern Skills Diploma for Adults (MSDA) with a £10m provision over three years (Press Release 28 June 2001).
- Passed legislation extending careers education to all pupils and students aged 16-19 attending most maintained schools, pupil referral units and Further Education institutions (Press Release 15 May 2001).
- Announced funding of approximately £300,000 under the Wales Union Learning Fund for 'Modern Employment Skills for Steelworkers under threat of Redundancy' project to help alleviate the suffering caused to Corus steel communities (Press Release 23 May 2001)
- Announced an additional £700,000 for the *Education IT Strategy* (Press Release 29 November 2000).
- Successfully lobbied Westminster to ensure that threshold assessors in Wales are employed by Local Education Authorities. In England private companies are used to assess teachers for performance related pay. In Wales, the money is given to LEAs thus keeping any profit within the education sector (Cf. The Pre 16 Education, Schools And Early Learning Committee Report To The Assembly for a précis of the teachers pay issue – June 2000).
- Created the General Teaching Council for Wales (Press Release 8 November 1999) .

Pensioners

- Announced £10m available over three years to take forward *the Strategy for Older People*, which is the first of its kind in the UK (Press Release 11 December 2002).
- Provided free dental checks for over 60s (Performance Report 2000 - 2001).
- Provided a platform for the formation of the All Party Group on Older People and Ageing. The purposes of the group include bringing together those with an interest in issues affecting older people and providing Assembly Members with a source of information and expertise on issues of age. The group has four

officers, one from each of the political parties represented in the Assembly.

People with Disabilities

- Announced new funding to help increase the participation in the arts in Wales, by the disabled. In recognition of the European Year of Disability in 2003 the Arts Council of Wales has been asked to operate a scheme that will support projects during and after the yearlong event. Almost £300,000 will be made available over three years (Press Release 31 October 2002).
- Made the latest digital hearing aids available on the NHS in Wales (Press Release 27 August 2002).
- Published distinctive guidance on the registration of care homes. The pattern of accommodation for people with learning disabilities in Wales is very different from England; small scale, not in units but in domestic style houses.
- Announced a one off grant to rescue the Cardiff Special Olympics UK. The National Assembly for Wales and Cardiff County Council each gave a £64,000 grant to stage the event in Cardiff (Press Release 11 July 2001).
- Welcomed the British Wheelchair Championships to Wales (Press Release 29 June 2001).

Health and Social Services

- Backed a motion which could lead to an end to smoking in all public places (Plenary 22 January 2003).
- Initiated work on the *Autism Strategy for Wales* (Press Release 4 December 2002).
- Helped highlight World Aids Day in Wales. It was stated in the press release that some 740 people have been diagnosed in Wales as having HIV (Press Release 1 December 2002).
- Launched a new scheme to provide a range of vision aids and appliances from high street opticians for people in Wales with low vision. Examples of low vision aids include stand magnifiers, hand magnifiers, pocket magnifiers, needles, needle threaders, liquid levellers and signature guides (Press Release 1 November 2002).
- Extended clinical training to Swansea (Press Release 27 September 2002) and announced plans to develop clinical schools in north Wales (Press Release 1 November 2002).
- Secured, through the *Care Standards Bill*, an independent *Commission for Care Standards* for Wales as an executive arm of the Assembly (April 2002).
- Froze prescription charges in Wales since April 2001 (Press Release 28 March 2002).
- Introduced incentives to help recruit and retain GPs, including a pioneering £5,000 'golden hello scheme' for newly qualified GPs coming to work in the NHS in Wales (Press Release 15 January 2002).
- Introduced a Care Council for Wales to regulate the social care workforce. According to the Care Council the social care profession employs over 70,000 people and is one of the most important service areas in Wales. Social care workers work to provide support to over 100,000 people at any given time in Wales. They provide a range of social care services enabling some of the most

vulnerable people in Wales to live as independently and safely as possible. The Council became operational in October 2001.

- Moved to change the structure of the NHS in Wales by scrapping the Health Authorities from 2003 and replace them with 22 Local Health Boards. (In Cabinet - July 2001).
- Introduced free nursing care for nursing home residents. The announcement stated that the model adopted for free nursing care was unique to Wales. The consultation process showed strong support for the Welsh model rather than the *banding system* introduced in England (Press Release 5 November 2001).
- Introduced a fairer funding formula for the NHS, which re-distributes a share of Wales' increased health funding to disadvantaged areas with the greatest health needs (Press Release 4 July 2001).
- Launched a *National Service Framework for Coronary Heart Disease* (Press Release 3 July 2001).
- Introduced the *Community Food Initiative* to help tackle the barriers to healthy eating and address issues of health inequalities (Press Release 27 October 2000).
- Initiated measures to improve the number and status of women, disabled people and ethnic minorities among the Health Service's 70,000 employees (*A Human Resource Strategy for NHS Wales* – Delivering for Patients NHS Cymru Wales June 2000).

Jobs and the Economy

- Launched an Innovation Action Plan (Press Release 26 February 2003).
- Helped gain the first ever major defence procurement contract for Wales bidding to supply a replacement battlefield radio communications system for the British Army at Oakdale Business Park near Blackwood (Press Release 8 November 2002).
- In October 2002, it was announce that more grant funding was accepted by businesses in Wales than any other region in the UK. The figures from the Department of Trade and Industry revealed that £109 million worth of RSA (Regional Selective Assistance) grant offers from the Assembly to 235 companies were accepted during the period between April 2001 to 31 March 2002. These grants, at the time, were forecast to lever in £430 million of private sector investment, create 7,700 new jobs and safeguard 4,000 existing jobs in Wales (Press Release 1 October 2002).
- Encouraged plans to reform the British Tourism Authority to strengthen the marketing of Britain and Wales overseas and to make the BTA much more accountable to the Assembly (Press Release 31 October 2002).
- Supported plans to create a multi-million pound film studio complex at Llanilid (Press Release 1 October 2002).
- Unveiled the location of Wales' first International Centre in New York (Press Release 23 September 2002).
- Developed Assembly Investment Grants for small businesses throughout Wales, offering support of £5000 - £50,000 (Press Release 19 June 2002).
- Announced £5.6 million for the Llanhilleth area regeneration scheme in Blaenau Gwent (Press Release 22 November 2001).
- Announced a £66 million package of remedial measures, through a

collaborative approach, to help rebuild the futures of the steelworkers and communities affected by the Corus closures and helped the majority of those who lost their jobs to find alternative work (Press Release 3 May 2001).

- Set up Careers Wales as a national all-age guidance service unique in the UK (Press Release 14 February 2000).
- Published a *National Economic Development Strategy* for the next 10 years – *A Winning Wales.*
- Announced an additional £1 million for the Welsh Development Agency to encourage Foreign Direct Investment (Press release 29 November 2000).
- Created a new Business Partnership Council (First Meeting 16 December 1999) and the Social Partners Unit to facilitate engaging with the private sector.
- Contributed to Wales' GDP by expanding its media, political advocacy, translation, and legal services capacity.

Poverty Eradication

- Created a new Child Poverty Task Group (Press Release 5 February 2003).
- Announced a public consultation on proposals for new valuation bands and proportions with the aim of delivering a fairer council tax system in Wales. This will be the first time that such a council tax revaluation and rebanding has been undertaken anywhere in the UK (Press Release 19 December 2002).
- Established the Community Loan Fund (CLF) operated through Finance Wales to help communities increase long-term sustainability. The Assembly has allocated almost £2 million to CLF over four years, which will be match funded by HSBC giving an overall budget of £4 million (Press Release 22 November 2002).
- Launched the Post Office Development Fund, a new £2.5 million fund to support post offices in deprived and/or isolated parts of Wales (Press Release 15 November 2002).
- Provided funding of up to £400,000 to refurbish the upper floor of the Swansea YMCA building to an appropriate standard to house a new unit for ex-offenders with substance misuse problems. The project is a joint venture involving YMCA-Swansea, the Salvation Army, Swansea Prison, the Probation Service, local authority and other stakeholders. Vulnerable prisoners will be offered the opportunity to spend six months in the supported accommodation after their discharge from jail, learning life skills to help them cope better with society at large (Press Release 6 November 2002).
- Announced unprecedented levels of support for Credit Unions throughout Wales by providing £1.4 million for a £3.5 million 3-year programme for growth. A Credit Union is a mutual organisation owned and run by its members for the benefit of its members. It offers an easy and convenient place to save, and gives access to low cost loans. It costs £1 (non-refundable) to become a member of a Credit Union and then you start saving as much or as little as you can afford. As soon as you start saving, you become a member (and part owner) of the Credit. Many members say it is the first time they have got into proper control of their finances (Press Release 10 July 2002).
- Announced the launch of a £9 million Community Trust Fund. Each Communities First area and Community of Interest supported under the

programme would be able to access up to £20,000 in each year. Smaller pockets of deprivation that are supported under the programme will be able to access up to £10,000 (Press Release 14 December 2001).

- Successfully committed more of its Objective One funds to projects than any of the English regions (Press Release 18 November 2001).
- Established a Health Inequalities Fund to tackle some of discrepancies in healthcare in Wales' poorest communities in July 2001.
- Introduced legislation extending the duties of local councils to accommodate 16 and 17 year old homeless people, care leavers, people made homeless because they were escaping from violence and people who became homeless following discharge from the armed forces or release from prison (*Homelessness (Priority Need) (Wales) Order 1 March 2001*).
- Announced an extra £1.1 million to the local government settlement for 2001-2002 to cover the preparatory costs of the Supporting People Measure (Press Release 29 November 2002).
- Set up a Homelessness Commission in November 2000.
- Led to the announcement, following the granting of additional Objective One money for Wales, that deprived areas in England would receive funding worth £600 million (Hansard 18 July 2000).
- Helped schools in socially deprived areas to combat social exclusion by transferring £1.5 million from the teacher restructuring budget line, where funds were deemed to be adequate, to the grants for education support and training (GEST) programme (Plenary 1 December 1999).
- Announced £3.6 million for Welsh local authorities to help tackle issues of rough sleeping and £0.4 million to the Sustainable Communities budget (Plenary 1 December 1999).
- Created a Community Investment Authority to channel funding to community and voluntary enterprises.

Equal Opportunities

General

- Made basic equality awareness training mandatory for 3,500 members of staff (Arrangements to Promote Equality of Opportunity 2001-2002 – June 2002).
- Introduced a training placement and work shadowing scheme for underrepresented groups in January 2002 (Arrangements to Promote Equality of Opportunity 2001-2002 – June 2002).
- Overseen several equality audits of the entire National Assembly civil service. Progress has been demonstrated through the increasing level of awareness of the importance of equality, the strong commitment to taking these issues forward, and the increasing engagement with a broader community (Arrangements to Promote Equality of Opportunity 2001-2002 – June 2002).
- Provided funding to establish a Welsh Local Government Association Equalities Unit. The team, led by Naomi Alleyne, is jointly funded by the Welsh Assembly Government and Welsh Local Government Association to support local authorities in making further progress on equality issues.½ Its main functions are to support the development of best practices in Welsh Local Government

and to provide advice and guidance on implementing the Equality Standard for Local Government in Wales. The unit was established during the Spring of 2002).

- Had the review of equality in its own pay structure described as best practice by the UK's Equal Opportunities Commission (Equal Opportunities Commission, (2001) *'Just Pay'*).
- Secured top-level civil service commitment to the equal opportunity work programme (Equal Opportunities Committee Annual Report 2000-01 – June 2001).
- Mainstreamed equality of opportunity into Objective One structural aid programme (Equal Opportunities Committee Annual Report 2000-01 – June 2001).
- Initiated a contract compliance contract that requires the suppliers of goods and services to the Assembly and its sponsored bodies to have good equality of opportunity practices (Equal Opportunities Committee Annual Report 2000-01 – June 2001).
- Linked the overall budget settlements that councils receive to performance against targets on equal opportunity (Equal Opportunities Committee Annual Report 2000-01 – June 2001).
- Had the Equal Opportunities Commission, Commission on Racial Equality and the Disability Rights Commission as standing advisers to the Assembly's Committee on Equal Opportunity.

Disability

- Celebrated the International Day of the Disabled People by holding a Plenary session for the Young Disabled people in Wales (Press Release 3 October 2001).
- Provided funding for Disability Wales and Wales Women's National Coalition to support dedicated staff, expand their membership and feed into policy consultations (Equal Opportunities Committee Annual Report 2000-01 – June 2001).
- Established the Learning Disability Advisory Group (December 1999).

Faith

- Concluded that the Assembly could make resources available to meet the demands of parents who wish to have their children educated in their own religion (Committee on Equal Opportunity Minutes 3 February 2000).

Gender

- Carried out a pay review and introduced a pay system which addresses gender pay inequity amongst its own staff. The Equal Pay Campaign was launched on 7 March 2002 (Arrangements to Promote Equality of Opportunity 2001-2002 – June 2002).
- Provided Wales with the only cabinet in the world where the majority of the members are women.

Language

- The Committee on Equal Opportunity underlined its concern about the lack of Welsh speaking non-executive directors on health authority and NHS Trust boards (Arrangements to Promote Equality of Opportunity 2001-2002 – June 2002).

Race

- Announced a grant of £325,000 for a new organisation providing support to black, minority ethnic (BME) people in Communities First Areas in Wales. The Black Ethnic Minority Support Team – BEST – brings together a number of existing organisations to help identify and engage BME communities and organisations with the Communities First programme (Press Release 11 December 2002).
- Assisted Wales's Ethnic Business Support Programme through the Assembly's WalesTrade International. The EBSP is a non-profit making company designed to help minority ethnic communities access mainstream business support agencies. It was announced in October 2002 that since June 2001, it had helped to start up more than 70 businesses in the Objective One and Two areas, creating over 200 new jobs and assisting nearly 250 individuals (Press Release 17 October 2002).
- Published an action plan to promote race equality in housing (Press Release 24 September 2002).
- Funded a short term secondee to the Welsh Refugee Council to take forward the implementation of the Home Office recommendations to ensure that asylum seekers in Wales have appropriate support (Arrangements to Promote Equality of Opportunity 2001-2002 – June 2002).
- Appointed the first senior civil servant in Wales from a minority ethnic background. He has been working on a range of issues including outreach to black and minority ethnic communities to improve their understanding of the Assembly and to promote good race relations in the light of the recent tensions occasioned by the terrorist attacks in New York and Washington (Press Release 18 October 2001).
- Held an Ethnic Minority Recruitment Fair, which was attended by 1,200 people (Press Release 11 April 2000).
- Undertook in partnership with the PCS union a review of institutionalised racism at the Assembly. From the review a number of recommendations were made. The most significant being a radical change in the manner in which the Assembly undertakes recruitment (Equal Opportunities Committee Annual Report 2000-01 – June 2001).
- Reviewed the provision of services for gypsy-travellers in Wales (Equality of Opportunity Committee Minutes 22 May 2002).
- Developed the newly formed All Wales Ethnic Minority Association to support dedicated staff, expand their membership and feed into policy consultations (Equal Opportunities Committee Annual Report 2000-01 – June 2001).
- Established a working group to consider how the recommendations of the Stephen Lawrence inquiry can be implemented in Wales especially through

achieving a multi-cultural approach in the school curriculum, giving guidance regarding racial harassment and imposing a requirement on education providers to monitor reported racial incidents (Equal Opportunities Committee Annual Report 2000-01 – June 2001).

- Sought to address the under representation of ethnic minorities in the Assembly by advertising far more posts than was the case under the Welsh Office (Equal Opportunities Committee Annual Report 2000-01 – June 2001).
- Announced free eye tests with a view to helping communities in Wales that experience specific health difficulties. Afro-Caribbean people are more prone to glaucoma and Indian, Pakistani and Bangladeshi people are more susceptible to diabetes and cataracts (Press Release 16 March 2000).
- Funded two NHS Race Equality Advisers (Press Release 10 August 2000).

Sexuality

- Welcomed the launch of the Lesbian, Gay and Bisexual Forum. It was stated in the Forum's Draft Business Plan in September 2002 that it was unique in being the only government sponsored forum for lesbian, gay and bisexual people in the UK. The National Assembly helped to finance the Forum through its Promoting Equality in Wales Project Development Fund. (Press Release 30 August 2001).

Volunteering

- Successfully lobbied the Home Office concerning the Criminal Records Bureau's Welsh language provision and moved to create an all Wales 'umbrella body' to help the voluntary sector process 'Disclosure' applications (Press Release 14 February 2003).
- Launched the Community Facilities and Activities programme, a one-stop source of funding for all community and voluntary groups across Wales (Press Release 18 October 2002).
- Provided a Capacity Fund of some £85,000 to enable voluntary networks to respond creatively to the work of the Voluntary Sector Partnership Council (VSPC Minutes 16 March 2001).
- Published annual reports on the *Voluntary Sector Scheme* which for the first time provided details of Welsh Assembly Government Funding for the voluntary sector and funding by Assembly Sponsored Public Bodies (ASPB).
- Announced an additional £700,000 for local voluntary groups and Volunteering in Wales, making the amount available for local voluntary groups in 2002-2003 around £2.5million (VSPC Minutes 14 December 2001).
- Provided a formal framework for the voluntary sector to comment on the Communities First Scheme, affecting some of Wales' poorest communities, through the Voluntary Sector Partnership Council. Since the launch of the programme in the June 2001, around £10 million had been allocated and by then almost £2 million had been spent (VSPC Minutes 14 December 2001).
- Presented the *Code of Practice on Funding the Voluntary Sector* (VSPC Minutes 19 October 2001).
- Enabled voluntary groups to plan their budgets better following a strategic

funding review (VSPC Minutes 22 June 2001).

- Brought Wales' faith communities closer together and to government through the new Inter Faith Council for Wales. The new Inter Faith Council nominates the faith communities' representative on the Voluntary Sector Partnership Council (Press Release 11 January 2002).
- Successfully conveyed the conviction of the voluntary sector to the Home Office that the fee for the Criminal Records Bureau checks should be free of charge for voluntary groups (Press Release 7 February 2001).
- Passed a *Voluntary Sector Scheme* which has acted as a catalyst for developing a recognition that the voluntary sector has an important part in the future of Wales (July 2000).
- Allowed representatives from Wales' voluntary groups unprecedented access to cabinet ministers every six months, to discuss issues such as local government funding, European funds, the Communities First Scheme and how Wales is receiving, or not, its share of non-devolved funding from Whitehall (July 2000).
- Allowed Wales' voluntary organisations a statutory access to government by the creation of the Voluntary Sector Partnership Council (July 2000).
- Created a new Voluntary Sector and Inclusion Division in the Welsh Assembly Government to reflect the importance of the Voluntary Sector.

Wales and the World

- Welcomed the opening of Amnesty International's new Wales office (Press Release 20 November 2002).
- Helped secure Bmibaby for Cardiff International Airport (Press Release 24 October 2002).
- Was the first UK legislature to provide a political platform for commemorating the Armenian Holocaust (Plenary Short Debate 16 May 2002).
- Successfully argued that national flags and symbols should be displayed on car number-plates. The UK Department for Transport, Local Government and the Regions, which has responsibility for vehicle registration regulations, initially expressed concerns about the ability of enforcement cameras to read number-plates with flags (Press Release 28 December 2001).
- Welcomed officials from countries seeking membership of the European Union who visited Wales on a fact-finding mission on regional policy. They met with National Assembly First Minister Rhodri Morgan for talks on regional policy in Wales before visiting UK Steel Enterprise – a project part-funded by the European Regional Development Fund which provides support to businesses in traditional steel areas of Wales. (Press Release 24 July 2001).
- Created a Cabinet Sub-Committee, with published minutes, on Wales and the World (First Meeting 30 April 2001).
- Successfully encouraged the USA to set up a consular presence in Wales in November 2000.
- Secured a voice for Wales in the developing European Constitutional Regions network which acts as a pressure group for regions with legislative powers. Wales a seat at the European table along with other European regional governments (Press Release 20 September 2000)
- Opened an Assembly office in Brussels in September 2000.

- Nominated the UK's representative on the Committee of Experts, which is responsible for monitoring how the European Charter for Regional or Minority Languages is implemented by signatory states. Countries who sign the Charter undertake to adhere to at least 35 paragraphs relating to measures in support of their languages. When the Charter was signed by the UK, at least 52 paragraphs applied to its measures in support of the Welsh language. (Press Release 5 October 2001).
- Announced an additional £100,000 from the budget for international relations (Press Release 29 November 2000).
- Encouraged the Department of International Development to take a more active role and interest in Wales, especially in supporting the educational aspects of international development in schools.
- Set up the all party Wales Overseas Agencies Group on international development.
- Allowed aid agencies to use the Assembly building and short debates to profile international debt cancellation programmes.
- Organised programmes (April 2000-March 2001) through the Assembly's Overseas Unit for 129 foreign delegations. 37 of the programmes were arranged on behalf of Foreign and Commonwealth Office.

Culture and Sport

- Successfully lobbied Westminster over the *Licensing Bill* . Whilst licensing is a non-devolved matter, provisions in the Bill would have had significant wide-ranging implications on several key policy areas which are the responsibility of the Assembly Government – the arts, community sustainability and social inclusion in particular (Press Release 18 February 2003).
- Announced a package of funding for the Brecon Jazz festival. The funding of up to £381,000 will help secure the longer-term future of the festival and to enable it to be staged in 2003 (Press Release 18 February 2003).
- Supported Cardiff's bid for the 2008 European Capital City of Culture nomination by providing over £1.1million (Press release 12 December 2002).
- Helped launch of the Wales Screen Commission as a new single national body to market the whole of Wales as an attractive and competitive film location to film makers and producers across the world (Press Release 20 November 2002).
- Announced that the final leg of the Wales Rally GB championship would remain in Wales for four years. The direct economic benefit has been conservatively estimated in excess of £50million (Press release 17 November 2002).
- Provided the necessary funding to save and display the Newport mediaeval ship for future posterity. Together with Newport City Council, the Assembly made a joint approach to the Heritage Lottery Fund to assist with the project, specifically for the treatment and conservation of the timbers (Press Release 23 August 2002).
- Ensured that review of the National Lottery announced by Secretary of State for Culture, Media and Sport, Tessa Jowell, will have a distinct Welsh voice (Press Release 29 July 2002).
- Helped secure, through new partnerships, the Ryder Cup 2010 for Wales through

- the Team Wales bid (Press Release 28 September 2001).
- Set up a Football Forum for Wales (Press Release 20 June 2001).
- Gave £500,000 to help bring the FA Cup Final to Cardiff (Press Release 10 May 2001).
- Established Cymru'n Creu as strategic body of organisations working to strengthen the cultural life and industries of Wales (Press Release 26 February 2001).
- Announced backing for the Wales Millennium Centre in January 2001.
- Announced an extra £60,000 for the National Museum for 2001-2002 to extend free admission to students and the disabled (Press Release 29 November 2000).

Environment Planning and Transport

Environment

- Launched a *Trunk Road Estate Biodiversity Action Plan* containing proposals for actions to be undertaken by the Welsh Assembly Government's Transport Directorate between 2004 and 2014 to safeguard species and habitats such as otters, Welsh clearwing moths and orchid rich grassland (Press Release 21 February 2003).
- Increased the number of Special Protection Areas for birds in Wales (Press Release 5 December 2002).
- Published in consultation with the Countryside Council for Wales and its partners, *The List of Species and Habitats of Principal Importance for Conserving Biological Diversity*, which includes 171 species and 40 habitat types (November 2002).
- At the Earth Summit, Johannesburg, Wales was one of the inaugural signatories of the Gauteng Declaration which commits regions around the world to share knowledge and best practice on Sustainable Development. Wales is also a leading participant in a pan-European network of regions on Sustainable Development (Press Release 2 September 2002).
- Passed regulations, following extensive consultations, to restrict the use of lead gunshot over wetlands in Wales. The UK has a commitment under the African-Eurasian Waterbird Agreement to endeavour to phase out the use of lead shot. Lead shot has been identified as posing a particular risk to waterfowl from lead poisoning, resulting from its ingestion when taking in grit to aid digestion (Press Release 30 August 2002).
- Ensured that Wales, through its First Minister, was represented at the Earth Summit in Johannesburg (Press Release 5 August 2002).
- Provided Wales with the first government in the world to use ecological foot printing as an indicator of real progress in sustainable development. The Wales Ecological Footprint is an indicator of how much of the world's resources Wales is using as it measures the productive land and sea area needed to support the way we live. (Press Release 17 April 2002).
- Through *Planning Policy Wales*, provided significant new guidance on biodiversity, particularly on community involvement in the Local Biodiversity Action Plan process and how these link into the planning process (Press Release 16 April 2002).

- Announced an additional £257,000 for Sustainable Development to begin work on the European Regional Innovation Grant Scheme (Press Release 29 November 2000).
- Successfully argued for a restrictive approach to the use of GM crops. Wales has the toughest regulatory regime possible in Genetically Modified Organisms (GMO). No trials of GMO crops currently being held in Wales; and the Assembly's action on separation distances between GM and non-GM crops generated debate and discussion within the European Union (Press Release 14 March 2000).
- Launched Tir Gofal, the all Wales whole farm agri-environment scheme. The first agreement was signed at Bedlwyncoch Farm, at Crai, near Sennybridge, on 14 March, 2000. A further expansion to Tir Gofal was announced in the Spring of 2002, with an additional £1.5m per year, on top of the year-on-year expansion programmed in the Wales Rural Development Plan. The 1000th Tir Gofal agreement was signed in October 2002. More recently, an extra £6.3 million was announced in 2004/05 – 2005/06 to continue the same expansion (Press Release 13 March 2000).
- Challenged the recommendation of the DETR-led review that the Environment Agency should remain an England and Wales body.

Planning

- Set up a Design Commission to oversee quality buildings and environments in Wales (Press Release 16 May 2002).
- Launched *Planning Policy Wales* offering a distinctive planning policy for future land use in Wales (Press Release 16 April 2002).
- Issued expanded guidance on where Green Belts and green wedge designations may be appropriate (Press Release 16 April 2002).
- Announced a package of measures to change the planning system regarding the location of mobile telephone masts around Wales. The Assembly, for example, introduced legislation to strengthen public consultation requirements on proposals for masts of 15m and below so that they are exactly the same as applications for masts above that height that need planning permission (Press Release 6 April 2001).
- Allocated an additional £3 million over three years for flood prevention measures (Press Release 29 November 2000).

Transport

- Launched the first *Road Safety Strategy for Wales* – which aims to help reduce the total number of people killed or seriously injured on Welsh roads by 40 per cent by 2010. (Press Release 23 January 2003).
- Encouraged the use of buses. It was announced that the number of bus passengers had increased since the introduction of the free travel scheme by 16% on average in south east Wales and 10% on average elsewhere (Press Release 20 November 2002).
- Announced an extra £10 million in each of 2002-2003 and 2003-2004 from the Capital Modernisation Fund for integrated transport projects (Press Release

29 November 2000).

Rural Wales and Agriculture

General

- Created a Cabinet Sub-Committee, with published minutes, on Rural Regeneration (First Meeting 28 October 2002).
- Announced the £3 million Rural Community Action programme to include help for rural retail services; rural community regeneration through local partnerships; funds to establish a Wales Rural Observatory; and funding to promote entrepreneurial skills for young people in rural areas (Press Release 23 October 2002).
- Initiated research on 'Age Balanced Communities' to address why young people leave rural Wales and also the difficulties of staying/returning. A review of all the relevant statistical and literature evidence is currently underway and arrangements are being established to collate new detailed evidence from six beacon community areas within: the Llyn Peninsula; North Ceredigion; Anglesey; Pembrokeshire; South Powys/North Monmouthshire; and Denbighshire (Age Balanced Communities' 12 August 2002).
- Announced a £65m funding package to support measures to help rural Wales recover from the effects of Foot and Mouth Disease. (Press Release 26 July 2001).
- Made sure that Wales' LEADER+ Single Programming Document, supporting rural projects, was the first of the UK's programmes to be approved by the European Commission. Currently, seven rural community groups are participating in the £9 million LEADER+ programme in Wales (the European Union initiative for Rural Development) (Press Release 4 July 2001).
- Led the way in the UK by recommending that the Office for Fair Trading should review the operation of the Code of Practice on supermarkets' dealings with food suppliers (Press Release 10 October 2000).
- Had its £450 million Welsh Rural Development Plan approved by the European Commission in autumn 2000.

Animal Health and Welfare

- Launched an *Animal Health and Welfare Strategy* (along with DEFRA and Scotland) to scope what people in Wales might want from such a strategy (Press Release 8 January 2003).
- Provided funding of £4m over 2 years to tackle a rise in bovine TB and, in co-operation with the State Veterinary Service, piloted new approaches to help eradicate the disease in Wales (Press Release 25 March 2002).
- Placed animal welfare concerns into the thinking behind the Tir Mynydd Scheme by making payments area-based. The scheme moves financial support away from intensive farming and grants per animal (Press Release 25 January 2001).

- Introduced the Welsh Ewe Genotyping Scheme (WEGS) in 2001 to increase resistance to scrapie in Welsh flocks; WEGS II, a three year £10.5 million programme to increase the scrapie resistance of the Welsh flock, launched for public consultation in January 2003 (Press Release 21 January 2003).
- The Geographical Information System (GIS) project has seen the Assembly create modern, up-to-date maps of all the registered farms in Wales. During the project in excess of 12000 farmers took the opportunity to meet with our staff to confirm the data held was correct. Currently the majority of the maps are in the final production stage and should be with all farmers by the end of February (Agriculture and Rural Development Committee Minutes 30 October 2002).
- Announced two pilot projects to help Welsh food producers and processors win local public sector business (Press Release 22 October 2002).
- Established Meat Promotion Wales, creating a more integrated structure for the development of red meat industry in Wales (Press Release 2 October 2002).
- Made progress in delivering the Wales Agri-Food Strategy, working through the WDA and the Agri-Food Partnerships. Over £16m committed in processing and marketing grant support over the last 18 months, supporting a total investment by food processing companies of £48m. (First Minister Annual Report 2001-2002).
- Made further improvements to the service provided to farmers on Common Agricultural Policy payments through the JIGSAW (Joint Initiatives for Government Services Across Wales) programme (Agriculture and Rural Development Committee Minutes 17 July 2002).
- Substantially improved arrangements for the Sheep Annual Premium agreed by the European Union in December 2001, nearly doubling payments to Welsh farmers (£83 million in 2002), and giving, for the first time, the National Assembly scope to determine how some of the money is spent in Wales, through the Welsh Sheep National Envelope (worth some £3.5 million annually) (Press Release 10 May 2002).
- Farm Improvement Grants and Farm Enterprise Grants have been introduced. The Assembly has approved in excess of 300 applications in total. This equates to £4.2m Improvement and £353,400 Enterprise grants being approved (Legislation Committee Minutes 29 January 2002).
- *Farming for the Future* was published in November 2001: the first ever strategy document setting a future direction for Welsh agriculture, reflecting the principles of sustainability (Press Release 21 November 2001).
- Published a monthly rural issues magazine *Gwlad* which is sent free to all farmers in Wales providing information on how to adapt farming businesses from Autumn 2001.
- Wales now has a much stronger voice in discussions in London and Brussels on the future of the Common Agricultural Policy. A full-time member of ARAD (Rural Affairs Department) staff, with diplomatic status, was appointed in Autumn 2001 to work in Brussels.
- Established an Independent Appeals Panel for farmers to adjudicate in

matters relating to agricultural subsidies and to assist in reducing the burden of paperwork on farmers (Press Release 5 October 2001).

- Provided matched funding to help the ARC Addington Fund distribute just under £3.5 million to Welsh farmers during the foot and mouth crisis (Press Release 30 August 2001).
- Stated clearly that Lord Haskins' comments, as head the government's recovery programme for England, concerning state hand-outs to farmers, were unhelpful and did not hold writ in Wales (Press Release 13 August 2001).
- Highlighted Welsh political frustration during the foot and mouth crisis with the Intervention Board's conduct of the welfare cull scheme and at not being able to follow Scotland's lead in easing restrictions (Press Release 2 August 2001).
- Successfully argued the case that UK beef producers should be exempted substantially from EU-wide cut-backs in beef production, agreed at the Agriculture Council in June 2001.
- Launched Tir Mynydd, a programme of support for hill farming - now worth some £36 million a year (Press Release 25 January 2001).
- Successfully argued the case of Welsh farmers in the changes to the financial support arrangements available under the Beef Special Premium Scheme (BSP). The 90-head limit on claims for Beef Special Premium was abolished, but with protection for small farmers (claims on up to 30 animals to be exempt from any scale-back caused by excess production). (Press Release 15 December 2000).
- Provided financial help (worth in excess of £600,000) to ease the burden of meat hygiene charges on small abattoirs, implementing the recommendations of the *McLean Report* (Press Release 28 November 2000).
- Raised concerns, in the context of CAP reforms, on the impact of degressivity (a steady year by year reduction of subsidy) on Welsh farmers (Agriculture and Rural Development Committee Minutes 21 June 2000).
- Secured full pound for pound matching funding from the UK Treasury for modulation of farm subsidies. The insistence of the devolved administrations on matching funding was crucial in achieving this (Agriculture and Rural Development Committee Minutes 21 June 2000).
- Successfully argued for a support package for farming as announced by the UK Government in March 2000 prioritising the livestock sector and giving a substantial three-year additional funding to hill-farmers½(Press Release 30 March 2000).
- Abolished dairy hygiene charges (worth £94 per farm inspection) and influenced former MAFF to take identical action in England (Agriculture and Rural Development Committee Minutes 9 February 2000).
- Criticised the Trade and Industry Secretary Stephen Byers for accepting the recommendation that Milk Marque should not be allowed to expand its processing capacity Press Release 3 August 1999).

isheries

- Successfully completed the Financial Instrument for Fisheries Guidance

Grant Scheme which provides finance measures for the adjustment of fisheries and aquaculture structures and the processing and marketing of their products (Voluntary Sector Grants – Current).

- Developed a hardship scheme to compensate cockle gatherers for loss of earnings during the closure of the Burry Inlet cockle fishery because of an outbreak of Diarhhetic Shelldish Poisoning (Written Questions Answered Between 17 and 24 October 2002)
- Announced that the Environment Agency (Wales) would receive £2.4m additional grant-in-aid, £800,000 a year for the next 3 financial years, to enable them to implement recommendations contained in the Review of Salmon and Freshwater Fisheries (Press Release 21 January 2002).
- Introduced Fisheries Objective 1 and non-Objective 1 schemes. It was announced, for example, that £203,253 would be granted to Gwynedd County Council to optimise the benefits of developing the sustainable use of fisheries in Gwynedd by restoring and improving fishery resources and angling facilities (Press Release 30 August 2001).
- Commissioned the Nautilus Study to identify potential opportunities for the sustainable economic development of sea and inland fisheries in Wales in March 2000. The intention was that the study would inform the Welsh Objective 1 and non-objective 1 fisheries programmes and would contribute to the co-ordinated socio-economic development of the coastal and rural Welsh economies (Agriculture and Rural Development Committee Minutes 16 May 2001).
- Introduced a licence database for the Importation of Live Fish from outside the UK.

Forestry

- Announced the £4m Cydcoed project in July 2001 to promote community facilities in woodlands and encourage community development, especially in areas with multiple deprivation. It was stated in December 2002, for example, that four projects had been agreed under the Cydcoed scheme in Pembrokeshire, namely the Slash pond walk in Broadhaven, which was receiving £28,000; the project in Clynfyw in Boncath, which was receiving over £100,000; Grove Junior School in Pembroke, which was receiving over £25,000; and Scolton Manor in Spittal, which was also receiving over £25,000 (Plenary 10 December 2002).
- Published the *Wales Woodland Strategy* with the Forestry Commission leading on implementation and advised by a wide-ranging Woodland Forum (Plenary 8 November 2001).
- Established 4 new mountain bike trail locations in Welsh woodlands building on the success of the trails in Coed y Brenin, helping to make Wales one of the top venues for mountain biking in the world (Agriculture and Rural Development Committee Minutes 19 June 2002)

The Welsh Language

- Announced an additional £1.5 million over 3 years for the development of a National Welsh Language Theatre (Press Release 16 December 2002).

- Unveiled a package worth £105,000 over three years to finance secondments of teachers of Welsh from Wales to Patagonia; training of local Welsh tutors and development of local Welsh cultural activities (Press Release 11 December 2002).
- Brought the Welsh Language Board's spending over three years to over £37 million (Plenary November 2002).
- Applied Objective One money to support the Welsh language. Announced nearly £390,000 for Mentrau Iaith Myrddin to create a network of five translators to work with community groups, voluntary organisations and community development agencies in Carmarthenshire (Press Release 9 May 2002).
- Supported the successful efforts of the Welsh Book Council to persuade a supermarket such as Tesco to sell Welsh Language books (Press Release 8 May 2002).
- Increased support for the Transference of Language in the Family Project (TWF) (Press Release 19 April 2002).
- Held a wide-ranging review of Welsh Language policy through its all-party Culture Committee in an effort to define in greater detail the stated aim of creating a bilingual Wales (Final Report Easter 2002).
- Forged new links with other bilingual cultures such as Canada in the context of creating law in two languages (Press Release 29 November 2001).
- Joined members of the Welsh Language Board in meeting with representatives from Language Boards of regional governments in Brussels. It was the first ever joint meeting of the Language Boards of lesser used European languages (Press Release 15 October 2001).
- Signed a new protocol with the province of Chubut. The settlement of parts of the Chubut province of Patagonia in Argentina by Welsh emigrants dates from 1865 (Press Release 19 June 2001).
- Guaranteed the National Eisteddfod £200,000 against any loss which could have been incurred following the foot and mouth outbreak (Press Release 14 June 2001).
- Compelled all local authorities to consider the Welsh language in drawing up their unitary development plans (Press Release 6 July 2000).
- Undertook a simultaneous review of the role of the Welsh Language in Education and Lifelong Learning looking specifically at Welsh medium and bilingual provision from Early Years provision to adult lifelong learning (Early Years Provision For Three Year Olds - Final Report for the Pre 16 Education, Schools and Early Learning Committee).
- Funded research into Welsh medium and bilingual provision for children and young people with Special Educational Needs and published a new SEN Code of Practice which includes a section on statutory obligations of Local Authorities under the *Welsh Language Act 1993*.
- Created law both in English and in Welsh.

Wales and the Law

General

- Since the advent of devolution the National Assembly has provided a degree of scrutiny over subordinate legislation which is unique in the United Kingdom.

It has the power not only to approve or reject subordinate legislation, but also to amend it in draft form. Westminster can only accept or reject draft legislation.

- Led to the establishment of the Office of the Counsel General for Wales. The National Assembly for Wales depends heavily on its in-house legal advice to fulfill its functions and to achieve its aims in a new, complex and immensely challenging political and constitutional environment. The Office of the Counsel General has been created specifically to provide that advice. The Counsel General is independent from UK Government Departments and independent of the Law Officers of the Crown.

Immigration

- Established links with the Immigration Services Commissioner and welcomed him to the Assembly (Committee on Equality of Opportunity Minutes 24 April 2002).

Law and Order

- Encouraged the formation of a new Advisory Committee on Criminal Justice (Press Release 22 August 2001).

Bringing the Law to Wales

- May have functioned as a catalyst for bringing the Mercantile Court, regular sittings of the Court of Appeal Civil Division, the Court of Appeal Criminal Division and regular sittings of the Employment Appeals Tribunal to Wales. The administration of justice in Wales has clearly been brought closer to the people since 1997.
- Coincided with the establishment of the Administrative Court of Wales, the Chancery Court in Wales, the Welsh Public Law Association and the Welsh Personal Injury Association.
- Helped launch Wales' first quarterly law journal (Press Release 8 August 2001)

Some Examples of Creative and More Accountable Government – Democratic Dividend

- The appointment, by the Assembly, of David Purchon as an independent investigator to the Nantygwyddon waste disposal site led to Rhondda-Cynon –Taff, Bro Taf Health Authority and the Environment Agency having to account for their actions to the affected local population. The local Council decided not to send household waste to the tip in December 2001 (Nantygwyddon Independent Investigation Minutes 1 May 2001).
- Resulted in the UK Treasury taking action to improve the transparency of the budgetary process by publishing a document outlining the categories of the devolved budgets over which there is scope for annual negotiation (1999).
- Provided an Audit Committee, held in open session and supported by the Auditor General for Wales and the National Audit Office, to ensure a greater

scrutiny over public expenditure and the management of issues such as the Cardiff Bay Barrage, clinical negligence in the NHS, Coleg Gwent and the proposed Assembly building.

- Pressed the case for the Auditor General for Wales to be allowed to audit limited companies, which spend public money.
- Led to witnesses from public bodies in Wales appearing more often before the Audit Committee than their English counterparts would before the Parliamentary Public Accounts Committee.
- Compelled civil servants to bring into the public domain questions such as formulating the new funding formula for Grants for Education Support and Training.
- Made Welsh politicians less dependant on political lobbyists through the appointment of expert advisers.
- Placed new farming support arrangements under far greater financial scrutiny by Assembly Members with farming backgrounds.
- Appointed Special Advisers through public adverts.
- Agreed to the inclusion of the National Council for Education and Training for Wales and the Higher Education Funding Council for Wales in the list of bodies subject to investigation by the Welsh Administration Ombudsman (November 2002). Inclusion in the list will enable individuals to take unresolved complaints to the Welsh Administration Ombudsman for review.
- Published budgets in an entirely new and radical way designed to promote inclusiveness and consensus. In the first Assembly budget, 29 of the 33 recommendations suggested by the subject committees were met.
- Enhanced the civil service's capacity by adding communications and policy functions to the Cabinet Secretariat bringing it into line with the Scottish Cabinet Secretariat.
- Merged the European affairs and industrial development divisions of the civil service into a single division to be driven more by policy priorities than administrative responses.
- Allowed local authorities in Wales greater freedom by not earmarking or hypothecating funds.
- Scrapped the *Best Value* regime designed to promote efficiency and high quality local government services, but regarded as bureaucratic, with a home grown Wales Programme for Improvement allowing authorities, rather than the Audit Commission, to conduct the analysis and ruled out any public branding of councils as 'good' or 'poor' performers.

Glossary of Terms:

ACCAC – Qualifications, Curriculum and Assessment Authority for Wales
APGID - National Assembly's All Party Group on International Development
ARAD – Assembly Rural Affairs Department
ASPB - Assembly Sponsored Public Bodies
BEST - The Black Ethnic Minority Support Team
BTA – British Tourism Authority
BSE - Bovine Spongiform Encephalopathy also known as "Mad Cow Disease"
CAFOD – Catholic Fund for Overseas Development
CEWC Cymru – Council for Education in World Citizenship Cymru
CJD - Creutzfeldt-Jakob Disease
CLF - Community Loan Fund
CRE – Commission for Racial Equality
CYMAD - A company which encourages the strengthening of communities (or cymunedau in Welsh) in Meirion, Arfon and Dwyfor. It covers an area which stretches from Aberdyfi in the south to Abergwyngregyn in the north.
DEFRA - Department for Environment, Food & Rural Affairs
DETR - Department of the Environment, Transport and the Regions
DFID – The Department for International Development
DPIA - Displaced People in Action
DTI – Department of Trade and Industry
EBSP - Ethnic Business Support Programme
ELWA - Council for Education and Training in Wales
ESTYN – Her Majesty's Inspectorate for Education and Training in Wales.
ECHR - European Convention on Human Rights
GEST - Grants for Education Support and Training
GDP – Gross Domestic Product
GIS - Geographical Information System
GMC - General Medical Council
GMO - Genetically Modified Organisms
HMP – Her Majesty's Prison
ILETS - International English Language Testing System
JIGSAW - Joint Initiatives for Government Services Across Wales
LGB - Lesbian Gay and Bisexual Movement
MSDA - Modern Skills Diploma for Adults
NHS – National Health Service
NRG for SD - Network of Regional Government for Sustainable Development
NGO - Non Government Organisation
PLAB – Examination to assess the professional and linguistic suitability of an overseas doctor to practice in the UK
RABI – Royal Agricultural Benevolent Institution
RFC – Rugby Football Club
SCF – Save the Children Fund
SCOVO - Standing Conference of Voluntary Organisations for People with a Learning Disability in Wales
TWF - Transference of Language in the Family Project
UNICEF – United Nations Children's Fund
UNCRC - UN Convention on the Rights of the Child
VSPC – Voluntary Sector Partnership Council
WASC - Welsh Affairs Select Committee
WDA – Welsh Development Agency
YMCA – Young Men's Christian Association

References

Better Wales (2000) National Assembly for Wales. Available from: http://www.wales.gov.uk/themesbetterwales/word/strategicplan_e.doc [Accessed 22 February 2003].

Better Health – Better Wales (1998) Presented to Parliament by the Secretary of State for Wales by command of Her Majesty May 1998. Available from: http://www.archive.official-documents.co.uk/document/cm39/3922/3922.htm [Accessed 22 February 2003].

Bobbitt, P. (2002) *The Shield of Achilles*. London: Penguin / Allen Lane.

Brierley, P. (2002/3) *Religious Trends 3, UK Christian Handbook*, ED., 2002/3.

Brown, G. (2000) *Hansard* 18 July 2000. Available from: http://www.publications.parliament.uk/pa/cm199900/cmhansrd/vo000718/debtext/00718-06.htm#00718-06_head0 [Accessed 22 February 2003].

de Oliveira, J.M. (1997) *Perception and Reality*. Available from: http://www.epub.org.br/cm/n04/opiniao/percepcao_i.htm [Accessed 22 February 2003].

Davies (2000), Lord G. P. Llanelli Eisteddfod Law Society Lecture

Dickey, B *Going About and Doing Good*, John Wolffe, *Evangelical Faith and Public Zeal*, London, SPCK, p. 54.

Gauteng Declaration. Available from: http://www.earthsummit2002.org/subnational/Microsoft%20Word%20-%20FINAL%20-%20The%20Gauteng%20Political%20Declaration%206-9-02.pdf [Accessed 22 February 2003].

Government of Wales Act 1998 (1998), The Stationery Office Ltd. London.

Griffith W.P. (2001), *Preaching second to no Other under the Sun, Religion and National Identity: Wales and Scotland c 17600-200,* Ed Robert Pope, Cardiff, University of Wales Press.

Ingram, K. (2001) Presentation by the Wales Funders Forum before the Voluntary Sector Partnership Council 16 March 2001. Available from: http://www.wales.gov.uk/themesvoluntarysector/content/partnershipcouncil/vspc01-1st-mtgnote160301-e.pdf [Accessed 22 February 2003].

Lost in Care - Report of the Tribunal of Inquiry into the Abuse of Children in Care in the Former County Council Areas of Gwynedd and Clwyd since 1974. Available from: http://www.doh.gov.uk/lostincare/20102a.htm [Accessed 22 February 2003].

National Assembly press releases are cited as accessed on 22 February 2003. Available from: http://www.wales.gov.uk/newsbysubject/index.htm [Accessed 22 February 2003].

Passing the Baton, Not Jumping Ship (2001) Community Care 6 December 2001. Available from: http://www.community-care.co.uk/articles/article.asp?liarticleid=34352&liSectionID=22&liParentID=26 [Accessed 22 February 2003].

Putting Wales First: A Partnership for the People of Wales - The First Partnership Agreement of the National Assembly for Wales 6 October 2000. Available from: http://www.wales.gov.uk/organicabinet/content/putting.html#3.%20Health%20and%20Social%20Care [Accessed 22 February 2003].

Ryder, J. (2001) Minutes- Committee on Equality of Opportunity 11 July 2001. Available from: http://www.wales.gov.uk/assemblydata/3B7159D100005D700000165500000000.pdf [Accessed 22 February 2003].

Sex and Relationships Education in Schools, National Assembly for Wales Circular No: 11/02. Available from: http://www.wales.gov.uk/keypublegislationcirculars/circulars/NAFWC11-02-e.pdf [Accessed 22 February 2003]

The Children's Society in Wales First Report, Select Committee on Welsh Affairs. Available from: http://www.parliament.the-stationery-office.co.uk/pa/cm200102/cmselect/cmwelaf/525/52504.htm [Accessed 22 February 2003].

Williams, P. (2000) *National Assembly Plenary* 28 March, 2000. Available from: http://www.wales.gov.uk/assemblydata/38E2287E000007B80000722900000000.pdf [Accessed 22 February 2003]

Williams R. (2002) Nations Markets and Morals *The Richard Dimbleby Lecture 2002*. Available from: http://www.bbc.co.uk/religion/news/archbishops/lecture.html [Accessed 22 February 2003].

UNICEF (2002) *The State of the World's Children 2002.*